why pray?

JOHN DEVRIES

why pray?

40 days – from words to relationship

MISSION
India

Grand Rapids, Michigan

Mission India
PO Box 141312
Grand Rapids, Michigan 49514-1312
877.644.6342
info@missionindia.org
www.missionindia.org

WHY PRAY?
Previously titled: *Does It Pay to Pray?*
© 2005 by JOHN F. DEVRIES
original © 1998, Mission India, Grand Rapids, Michigan

ISBN 978-0-9788551-5-4 (Agriculture soft cover)

(Previously published by Honor Books, and imprint of
Cook Communications Ministries, ISBN 1-56292-278-5)

First Printing, 2005

3 4 5 6 7 8 9 10 Printing/Year 15 14 13 12

Design by Julie Folkert

Library of Congress Cataloging-in-Publication Data

DeVries, John F.
  [Does it pay to pray?]
Why pray? : from words to relationship / John F. DeVries.
      p. cm.
ISBN 1-56292-278-5 (hardcover)
1. Prayer. 2. Prayer--Meditations. 3. Spiritual exercises. I. Title.
BV215.D45 2005
248.3'2--dc22
                                        2004026771

To our four children, their spouses,
and our grandchildren,
with gratitude and praise
for making their homes into
homes of prayer every day.

Dr. John DeVries is the founder of a Christian non-profit organization called Mission India. You will notice frequent references to the people of India in this book. You will also sense his deep love for India and his intense desire to reach its people with the glorious news that Jesus Christ loves them. John invites you to visit the Mission India website at www.missionindia.org. Please contact us at (877) 644-6342 or info@missionindia.org if you would like to learn more about Mission India.

PO Box 141312
Grand Rapids, Michigan 49514-1312

contents

WEEK ONE: WHY PRAY?

WEEK TWO: WHY PRAY FIRST?

WEEK FIVE: THREE FOUNDATIONS AND THREE FUNCTIONS OF A HOME OF PRAYER

EPILOGUE: BUILDING A HOME OF PRAYER EVERY DAY

foreword

You hold in your hands a small book that has the potential to revolutionize your prayer life! Yes, I know that countless volumes, some of them large, have been written on prayer, but this book is unique.

First, it is practical. John DeVries does not answer all of our theological questions about prayer, but he is interested in helping us take seriously the exercise of faithful intercession. In his matter-of-fact style, he is telling us that God actually does answer and if we are faithful, the Almighty will respond in ways that we have not thought possible. This book is excellent for beginners in the school of prayer, but it also is helpful for those of us who have taken prayer seriously for many years. Here is a simple plan for motivating us to do what we know we should, and to do it better!

Second, this book stresses what we need to hear: the purpose of prayer is not so much to get answers from the Almighty as it is to have fellowship with the Almighty! The illustration of the grandchild who delights his grandparents by his friendship and not by how much he can do is worth the price of the book! John knows that many of us become discouraged because we do not get answers to our prayers; we would be better served if we were to enjoy the *presence* of God rather than the *presents* from God!

Third, the power of this book is demonstrated by the lifestyle and experience of its author. When I met John perhaps fifteen years ago, I was impressed by his simple commitment to prayer and how he was assured that God would respond. And when I learned more about his missionary work in India, I realized that he was speaking about prayer from his own life and ministry.

More recently, I had the privilege of being with John at a Bible conference and hearing of the great advance of the Gospel through Mission India, founded by John. Once again, I was led to marvel at God's goodness in answering prayer as churches are being established throughout the land. One example after another was given of the difference that prayer makes.

John Bunyan, in his book *Pilgrim's Progress*, says that when Christian went knocking at the gate of the castle, the barking of a dog frightened him and he stopped knocking. Just so, when we knock on the door of heaven, it is easy to be distracted and back off. This little book reminds us that we must continually come to the Throne of Grace, even when the initial answer appears to be no.

In my own life I've learned that we need constant stimulation and encouragement in our prayer life. It is really true that prayer is always a battle, and that we must "persevere" if we are to see the victories we desire. This little book will help us keep looking to the Lord and help us remember that although we come to the Lord occupied with our need, we must leave off occupied with our God.

Don't read this book in one sitting; better to read a few pages a day and practice what you've read. Remember, "Prayer Changes Things."

ERWIN LUTZER, *Moody Church, Chicago*

preface

Why pray? John DeVries teaches us that prayer is something far more profound than merely a tool to get something from God. Prayer is a relationship. Prayer is "beyond words." Prayer is the primary expression of our love for God. We pray because we have been born again to a new life in Christ, and the primary expression of that new life in Christ is a living relationship with Him expressed in prayer.

In this book, DeVries encourages us to **H.O.P.E.**: to make our homes "**H**omes **O**f **P**rayer **E**very day," and through such a prayer *relationship* with our Savior bring hope to our families. Hope is expectation. Peter tells us that we are born again to a living hope. To pray is to live in a relationship of exciting expectation as we wait to be continuously surprised by our Lord and Savior. We bring H.O.P.E. to our home when we make it a home of prayer every day!

acknowledgements

This book would not have been possible without a myriad of people from whom I have learned much about prayer. Leading the list is my wife, Adelaide. In our over 50 years of marriage, we have built our own "**H**omes **O**f **P**rayer **E**very day." But there have been many others on our prayer pilgrimage, not the least of which were the many with whom we met every morning at 7:00 A.M. for prayer these past twenty years. I'm also grateful to the thousands of "India Intercessors" who pray for our ministry daily. So much of what I have learned about prayer has been taught by our Indian staff (Chirie, Kamala, and so many other fantastic prayers in India), and the many partner missions and churches that they serve. Their passionate prayer lives have often left me feeling a spiritual midget. I have so much to learn.

I think of my dear, late friend Ken Holtvluwer, and his wife June, with their passion for missions and dedication to prayer, who for over twenty years began each day in prayer with us. And I think of the others who so faithfully joined us in prayer, such as Arnie and Mary Lynn (now in eternity with the Lord).

Most of all, glory and praise to my Lord Jesus Christ who has made a small beginning in teaching me to pray. How I look forward to that day when communication and relationship with Him will be made perfect.

introduction

I have found that prayer comes more naturally to Eastern people than to Western people. I am not certain why this is but I have found new converts in India, without any training and direction, make their homes into **H**omes **O**f **P**rayer **E**very day. They do it naturally. Perhaps this happens because they live in a prayer culture that values dependency on family and on gods. We live in a self-sufficient culture that values independent thinking and living.

I believe that we limit ourselves to a boring and predictable life when we eliminate God's surprises in answer to our prayers and ask Him merely to bless our plans. God loves surprises, and the only certainty He desires in our lives is that we be certain of Him. I often think that we don't know more about heaven because God, like a parent at Christmas, wants to surprise us and won't tell us what is in His eternal present, reserved for us. Prayer is a love *relationship* with God in which we present our needs and then live in exciting, trust-filled wonder and anticipation of the unexpected ways that God will work. We are certain only of the fact that He will work in wondrous ways. What He does is always beyond anything we can ask or imagine (see Eph. 3:20).

This book will help you lead your family into new dimensions of prayer. True, effective prayer and hope (anticipation) always go hand in hand. Thus, we have a simple acronym—H.O.P.E. When you make your home a "**H**omes **O**f **P**rayer **E**very day," you will bring **H.O.P.E.** to your family. The forty meditations in this book help you understand the unique relationship between hope and prayer. The book is divided into five weeks and concludes with a five-day epilogue. It can be used in family devotions or in small-group study. The goal is to assist you in making your home a home of prayer every day.

The first week's devotions cover the importance of prayer. In this section we learn about praying *because of who God is* and *because we are made in His image.* God calls us to pray—in fact, prayer is a natural relationship between God and human beings.

The second week's devotions are about *priorities* in prayer. Too often we confuse our priorities. When we should be walking and talking with God, we're racing off to something that seems very important at the moment. Instead of praying, we deal with little emergencies, agonize over problems, create plans, and throw ourselves into projects. Even churches and mission groups lose their sense of direction from time to time!

During the third week we focus on praying for our neighbors. Too often neighbors wind up on the *bottom* of our prayer list. We ought to heed the prophet Samuel's words of caution: "Far be it from me that I should sin against the Lord by failing to pray for you" (1 Sam. 12:23). Praying for neighbors is so important that failure to do this is actually a sin against God! Could it be that the evils in our cities—crime, violence, family deterioration, and problems in schools—are due in part to the fact that we aren't praying faithfully for our neighbors?

In the fourth week we consider the question,

"How should we pray?" It's interesting that when Jesus' disciples had the opportunity to ask their Lord for some special training, after being with Him for almost three years, they chose the topic of *prayer*! "Lord, teach us to pray," they asked. Jesus responded by giving them an outline of a conversation with God—an outline we now call the *Lord's Prayer*. Like any conversation between friends, the Lord's Prayer is made up of four parts: (1) a "warm-up" period in which one person lets the other know he is interested in him and is excited about being there; (2) a time of sharing; (3) a time of reacting; and (4) a conclusion or "wrap-up." In the last seven devotional readings we explore this outline and walk with God through the conversation described by God's own Son.

In the fifth week we see what the person who prays becomes: namely, a royal or ruling priest. In the epilogue we review five simple steps toward making your home a home of prayer.

As you read through the forty daily devotionals in this book, you'll notice that each reading concludes with an idea to spark discussion as well as a brief topic for meditation. These "rest stops along the way" are valuable for personal reflection or for use as discussion starters in family devotions, prayer groups, home Bible study groups, or Sunday school classes.

I wish you a wonderful journey. May you be just like little Andrew in the devotional reading for Day 2. Sit on God's lap and feel His strong arms enfold you!

—*John DeVries*

why pray?

DAY 1

Does it pay to pray?

He was a very serious man, and the question he asked me was well-intentioned: "Does it pay to pray?"

Being a businessman, he knew he could not keep his business running smoothly unless he continually asked, "Does it pay…?" Many of his friends were out of business because they had failed to ask that question. So it was natural for him to pose this question to me, after what had been happening in our church.

For six months I had been challenging the church, as its pastor, to join me every morning at seven o'clock, seven days a week, for prayer. To my surprise, fifty-six people had shown up the first morning, and soon afterward the number had settled down to thirty or forty regulars. We experienced thrilling times as we saw 27 answers to our prayers and carefully tracked them for the rest of the church to see. One week we tallied forty-nine distinct answers to prayer!

But then something happened. It seemed as if God had turned off the power supply! We prayed and prayed, but no answers came. It soon got so bad that we hardly dared to pray for anything. It seemed as if we got the *opposite* of what we requested! If a couple was having marital trouble and we prayed for them, it seemed they were certain to get a divorce. If someone was seriously ill and we prayed, it seemed inevitable that he or she got worse or even died. Several members of the prayer group suffered terribly with sickness and family problems.

It was in this context that my friend asked, "John, does it pay to meet at church every day to pray?"

I was stunned because I had been growing disillusioned with prayer and confused with God. Before we started our prayer program, I had thought that if we prayed as the Christians in Korea had done, surely God would do for us what I thought He had done for them: our church would expand; we would see miracles; amazing things would happen. Never did I expect that when we prayed, the very opposite of what we asked for would happen. I thought for a moment about my friend's question and replied, "I guess it doesn't matter!"

"If it doesn't matter, why do you do it?" he asked.

"Because there must be some other reason for praying than that it pays!" I answered.

Since then God has shown me that my answer was from Him. If I were to respond to my friend today, I would ask him, "Does it pay to talk to your wife?"

Think about it.

The immediate answer is "Of course! Think of how troubled our marriage would be if we didn't talk!"

But let me press the question further: "Do you talk to your spouse *because it pays* or *because of love*?" You see, if you talk to someone only because it pays, you're doing it for a selfish reason.

When we view prayer in terms of the number of

answers we get, and when we track our answers in prayer journals just to be sure our time is well spent, are we not wrecking our relationship with God? Do you evaluate every conversation with your spouse or with a dear friend in terms of what you get out of it?

Consider the relationships in your life: friends, spouses, companions. Any positive relationship with another is a source of hope. To that end, when someone close dies, we feel "hopeless" in the sense that we cannot hope for a future with that person, at least in this life. Living love relationships provide hope, meaning, and significance to our lives. And the ultimate love relationship can be—must be— the one we have with God.

This is why we must never "prostitute" prayer, degrading it (and our perception of God) into some mechanical program for getting our way. Rather, prayer must be as living and natural and exciting as sharing our hearts with a friend. We must broaden our understanding of prayer if we wish to make our home a home of prayer every day.

Reflect/Discuss:
Do you tend to look at prayer in terms of answers rather than as an ongoing relationship with your closest friend?

Meditate:
Prayer is not a program but a relationship.

Prayer is sitting on God's lap

My wife and I are blessed with thirteen grandchildren (as of this writing). The oldest is ten, and ten of them are boys! In that crowd is six-year-old Andrew, whose other set of grandparents, Nanna and Poppa Dykstra, are dairy farmers in Nova Scotia.

When he turned six, Andrew spent a week with Nanna and Poppa Dykstra on their farm, "helping" in the barn and on the tractor. Of course Nanna and Poppa doted on him, as loving grandparents will, telling Andrew they just couldn't imagine how they got along on the farm without him!

When he left at the end of the week, their accolades rang in his little ears, and his head was swollen with pride—how he had helped them! They called regularly, and each phone call ended with talking to Andrew and asking when he could possibly get back to the farm to help out. It was so hard without him, they said, although they were getting by—but they could hardly wait!

Well, the little fellow took this seriously —so seriously that in his prayer circle at Sunday school he offered lengthy prayers asking God to help Nanna and Poppa because they had so much trouble running the farm without him.

How my wife and I laughed when our daughter, Mary, told us this story! Then God nudged me a bit, saying, "John, you've been like little Andrew with Me! You've treated Me like a helper in the sky, thinking that all the work has fallen on your shoulders. You laugh, in love, at your little grandson's inflated ideas of how he is needed on the farm, but don't you think that I, with love and delight, have laughed at all your exaggerated and puffed up ideas of importance in My kingdom?"

Since then, I have often thought of little Andrew on Poppa's lap as they lumbered off on the tractor to do some field work. This image strikes me as a picture of myself in prayer. Prayer is the dependent relationship in which I sit on the lap of my heavenly Father and put my hand on His as He steers the tractor. After all, He not only owns and drives the tractor, but He also owns the farm! And when the old Enemy, Satan, plays tricks on my mind, tempting me to think I don't matter to God, I ask myself what experiences on the tractor must have been most memorable for Poppa Dykstra. The answer, of course, is that of all the hours spent on the tractor, none were so precious as when he had his little Andrew on his lap and together they drove out to work in the field. As my heavenly Father looks back, surely the moments of greatest delight in His relationship with me were when I, in childlike dependence and faith, climbed into His lap in prayer, put my little hand on His big hand, and said, "Father, could we drive the tractor over here?"

God warns me, as Poppa Dykstra warned Andrew, "Don't ever get on the tractor alone! I want you on the tractor, but only when I am with you!" In other words, don't try sitting alone in the driver's seat of your life. See yourself in a prayer relationship, in a relationship of dependency, trusting God to guide you.

The fields that are ripe for harvest are God's. He owns the tractor, and He knows where to plow. Only when we, like little children, climb into God's lap in prayer, feel His arms of love around us, and experience the security of having our hands on His while He guides the steering wheel—only then will missions move!

I've had Andrew and other grandchildren on my own lap while mowing my lawn with a borrowed tractor. Feeling so comfortable and secure, more than once they've fallen asleep as we are riding. If you sometimes fall asleep in prayer while you are "sitting on God's lap," don't worry or feel as if you've disappointed God. If your Father needs you, He will wake you. Your quiet heart is a joy to Him. Prayer is meant to involve the same delight a little child feels on a grandfather's lap—and so much security that you might drift off to sleep!

Reflect/Discuss:

In what ways are you like Andrew, believing that his grandma and grandpa could not get along without him on the farm?

Meditate:

Prayer is a delightful position of dependency on God.

Prayer is holding hands with God

Prayer is not the ultimate program by which we get God to do things our way. It's like the act of a little child climbing into the lap of the Father and putting his hand on the hand of the One who is driving. And it's more. It's something far deeper—this mysterious relationship that is so much more than a means to get what we want. We were made and redeemed to pray. Prayer is a relationship in which we first of all recognize who God is and how greatly He is to be praised (see Ps. 48:1). And prayer is the means by which we do that. All of our communication with God is prayer. In prayer we are enfolded into God, and God is enfolded into us.

It's like this: when God made us, He made us in His image. This means, among other things, that we "look like" or resemble God in striking ways. Let's imagine that your left hand represents God and your right hand represents you. The two hands look like each other, but they're not the same, are they? Similarly, while we may look like God in some ways, as His image bearers, we are not the same as God.

We were made to bear God's image so that we might "fit into" God. You can picture this by fitting your hands together with your fingers interlocked and your palms open. Only human beings, who were made in God's image, can "fit into" God in a way like this. No animal or other creature can "fit into" God.

Something happened, though, in the way we "fit into" God. In our picture of the hands fitting together, think of the right hand becoming infested with thorny burrs stuck between each finger. The right hand has to be separated from the left hand, of course, because the "fit" is too painful. The right hand symbolizes us, and the burrs symbolize our sin. When Adam and Eve sinned, the pain of sin separated their "fit" with God. As long as sin remained, they could not be joined together with God.

Now, if we are that thorny right hand, there's no way for us to pull out those thorns! A right hand cannot get thorns out of itself. It needs the help of the left hand. So it is with our sin and us. There's no way we can get sin out of ourselves, so we need God, our "other hand," to do it for us. And that's exactly what God has done. In mercy, God freed us from our thorny sin so that we could fit together with Him again. God did this by sending His perfect Son, Jesus Christ, to take away our sin and give us new life. Think of the crown of thorns Jesus wore on the cross. Just as that crown was pressed upon His head, so our sins (thorns) were laid upon Him.

Hold your hands in the traditional way of folding hands in prayer. Think of your left hand as God and your right hand as yourself. Every time you pray, you are enfolded into the very heart of God.

This intensely close, intimate relationship is the deepest and most profound relationship any human being can have. It is far more intimate than any relationship we can have with another person. We can only be "externally" linked to another person, for we can never crawl into the mind of even those who are closest to us, those whom we love most dearly. Our relationship with God, though, is much different. The Holy Spirit, who searches the mind of God, comes to live in us! "Who among men knows the thoughts of a man except the man's spirit within him? In the same way no one knows the thoughts of God except the Spirit of God. We have not received the spirit of the world but the Spirit who is from God, that we may understand what God has freely given us" (1 Cor. 2:11–12).

Think of it: God's Spirit, who searches and knows the mind of God (as our spirit searches and knows our mind), is also in us! Prayer is the most intense, the most intimate moment of being enfolded into God's Spirit so that we are one with Him in thought and mind! It's the moment when, as the British preacher Oswald Chambers commented, we move from the plane of living by common sense to living on the supernatural level.

Reflect/Discuss:
Think of a moment when you were utterly overwhelmed and excited about the presence of God. Then tell someone about your experience.

Meditate:
Prayer is a dependent relationship with God in which I am enfolded into Him.

Prayer is filling the gas tank

I drive a rather old car with 130,000 miles on it—a big car that "floats" down the highway. I don't like the newer SUVs. They ride too hard. It may be fashionable to drive them, but I am old enough that I don't need to be fashionable. I can say I like to float rather than bounce down the highway. I really don't care what other people say.

Imagine that it's Sunday morning about ten minutes before worship time at your church and that I'm going to be preaching there. You notice me pushing a big old car down the road. It dawns on you that I am the guest preacher, and it's clear that I'm never going to arrive on time. I'm right in front of an open gas station about a five minute drive from the church and I'm passing the station! You slam on your brakes, hop out of the car, and ask me,

"What's the matter? Why are you pushing your car?"

I brush some perspiration off my forehead and reply that my car happens to be out of gas. "Why, then, are you pushing it past the gas station?" you ask. "Push it into the station, and fill it up!"

"But," I protest, "I don't have time to stop for gas. I have only ten minutes left to get to church. I can't be distracted by anything. I must be on my way!"

My reply is so foolish that it's hard to comprehend. No one in his right mind would be too busy to fill up if he were out of gas. No one would push his car past a gas station because he was in a hurry to get somewhere.

Think of this illustration whenever you want a good example of a prayerless Christian. The vast majority of Christians in our society claim they don't have time to pray. But that excuse is as senseless as my saying I don't have time to stop and fill my gas tank.

Prayer is the relationship in which we stop, right where we are, and are filled with the Holy Spirit. Without Him we can do nothing. "Remain in me, and I will remain in you. No branch can bear fruit by itself; it must remain in the vine. Neither can you bear fruit unless you remain in me" (John 15:4). Just as a branch apart from the life of the vine is fruitless, so we are empty apart from the indwelling presence of the Holy Spirit. Although the Spirit of God is given to every believer upon being born again—for there is never new life apart from His presence—there are many descriptions of being filled with the Holy Spirit in exceptional ways (see Luke 1:15; 4:1; Acts 2:4; 4:8, 31; 7:55; 11:24; 13:9, 52). The distinction made in all these passages—namely, that these people were filled with the Holy Spirit—is a distinction over other Christians who had the Holy Spirit but did not give evidence of that kind of filling. We are called to cooperate with the Holy Spirit, neither resisting nor grieving Him, so that every aspect of our being may surrender to and be saturated with His holy presence.

The Holy Spirit's power flows into us during regular times of prayer and praise. Jesus told us, as we will see in more detail later in this book, that we are to be "yoked" to Him—and when that happens, His power flows into us (see Matt. 11:29–30). The "yoke" of which He speaks is the "yoke" of prayer. As we open our minds and hearts in focusing our thoughts on God in petition and praise, we open up our entire beings, every aspect of our nature, to the filling of the Holy Spirit, who thus empowers us. Prayer, then, is far more than merely a relationship, even more than a dependent relationship upon God. It is a relationship of empowerment. In simple language, it is the time when our spiritual gas tank is filled with the power of the Spirit of God.

Reflect/Discuss:
Describe times when you prayed and did not feel empowered but rather felt as weak and limp as when you started. Why didn't the power flow?

Meditate:
Prayer is not a program but a dependent relationship upon God, through which we are empowered and filled by His Holy Spirit.

Prayer is being the friend in the middle

The words, spoken with a heavy southern drawl, still ring in my mind. My good friend Dr. Wilson Benton proclaimed, "We are to be friends in the middle in the middle of the night!" That was his interpretation of prayer, based on Luke 11:5–13.

In that passage Jesus tells us that prayer is like a friend in the middle. A person opens his home at midnight to a hungry friend who has been on a long journey. Out of courtesy the friend must feed this traveler, but there is no bread in his house. So he goes to the house of a wealthy friend who surely has bread, knocks hard on the door, and wakes him from a deep sleep, shouting that he needs bread. The wealthy friend is irritated and tries to send the noisy neighbor away, but the man continues shouting. Finally the wealthy friend has no choice but to get up and give the bread to the man and send him on his way. This is a parable about prayer, for it tells of our position in relation to the needs of the world, our inability to meet those needs, and our link to the One who can meet them.

The needs. The friend in the middle, or the middleman, was compelled to act. He could not ignore his friend's need for food. Not only did he have to be hospitable, but apparently he was moved by his friend's need. He felt so deeply about it that he did not want to leave it till morning. It was something he had to act on right away.

People who pray have developed not only a relationship with the Father but also a deep sense of the needs in their Father's world. They see these needs with broken and compassionate hearts. Harold Lindsell observed at Billy Graham's twenty-fifth anniversary of crusade ministry that the measure of spiritual maturity is not in the heights of ecstasy Christians achieve in worship but rather in the pain of a broken heart over the agony and needs of the world. Lindsell urged the audience to join the company of the brokenhearted and to stand with Jesus as He wept over Jerusalem. A person who is in a living prayer relationship with God is also in a living, painful relationship with the needs of the world! It is impossible to be in good standing with God without seeing around us the heartaches that God sees.

Our inability to meet the needs. Why do we so often look away from the needs around us? Because we are unable to meet those needs. In Acts 3:1–10 Peter and John looked a lame beggar straight in the eye; they could look at his need because they knew what to do about it. They knew that in themselves they couldn't meet the man's need. But they knew they could take it to God and that the power of Jesus' name could heal him.

How often do you look away from the family quarreling down the street or the problems of your inner city because you have little confidence in your relationship with the Source of all blessing? We are crippled not only by our inability to meet needs but also by our lack of faith that God will meet those needs. And much of the time we don't bring those needs to Him in prayer.

The joy and excitement of being a follower of Christ is found right here: in being able to look at the needs of the world and to know you have something significant to give toward every single need!

Knowing Who can meet the needs. The middleman gave what he had—namely, his relationship to his wealthy friend. He went to the wealthy friend in urgency knowing that the need had to be met, confident that this person had bread and would share it.

Near my home is an inner-city apartment complex of a hundred units. They are filled mainly with fatherless families and illegal immigrants. Crime was so high that the police responded to fifteen calls there every day.

But seven senior women in a neighboring church decided to become "friends in the middle" by praying for that housing complex. They began intensive prayer, and as a result, two years later, the police reported less than fifteen calls for an entire summer! Much happened, of course, to bring about this amazing answer to prayer, but it was the "friends in the middle" in the form of seven elderly women who started the flow of blessings. They could never minister on-site in such a situation, but they could pray.

Reflect/Discuss:
What situations have you seen that are beyond your ability to solve? Have you been a "friend in the middle," linking those needs with God? If not, why not?

Meditate:
Prayer is a dependent relationship in which we are empowered and enfolded into God and in which we link our needs to God's infinite resources.

DAY 6

Prayer is traveling with God

It's a lot more fun to travel with friends than to travel alone. I've spent many wearisome days on the road, and when traveling alone, I have virtually no motivation to take in the sights. The motto is, "Get the work done and get home!"

Then there are those days when my wife goes with me, and suddenly there's a new interest in discovering that little out-of-the-way restaurant and spending a few hours sightseeing. It's so much better when you can share it with someone! We get into an area of beautiful scenery, and the conversation goes like this: "Look over here; did you ever see anything like it?" Why is it that when we discover something unusual, our first inclination is to share it with our loved ones? The pain of losing loved ones is often intensified when we want to share some new discovery with them and we suddenly realize that sharing with them is no longer possible.

Prayer is like a "traveling" relationship with God. Travelers are filled with hope—with excitement, they anticipate new discoveries, new scenery, new towns. We are to have this kind of anticipation, wonder, and hope as we travel through life with God. In our homes, we should be sharing new discoveries about God constantly, not only in our studies of the Bible, but in our life experiences as well.

He loves to share the scenery with us, and He delights when we call His attention to what we see. One of the most remarkable moments of prayer in my life occurred this way. We had taken a midwinter vacation in northern Michigan several years ago. We were ice fishing and sledding with our children and decided to visit Tahquamenon Falls in Michigan's Upper Peninsula. The day dawned uncharacteristically bright for that time of year, and as we traveled up to the bridge linking the two peninsulas, we were constantly surprised by how God had graced the barbed wire fences with diamond-like necklaces of frozen dew, which sparkled brilliantly in the morning sun. The sparkling necklaces were not limited to the fences, but in His lavish way the Creator draped them from the roadside weeds, thistles, and trees as well.

As exciting as our trip there was, nothing could compare to the spectacular display of the Falls itself. Fresh snow, at least a foot deep, weighed down giant pines and made them bow before their God. We were the first to break through the crusted snow that morning as we pushed our way down the path. And when we rounded the corner in full view of the Falls, the sight was breathtaking. There before us was a giant icicle into which God had frozen all the brilliant colors of the rainbow. I shall never forget standing there and then bursting into laughter as I said, "God, if we humans had built this thing, we would be charging admission and making a mint. But here, tucked way back in the wilderness, You create for Yourself a picture of unsurpassed beauty. And then in two months You'll melt the whole thing, cause life to sprout and grow around here, and create another breathtaking scene. Then in the fall You'll splash color all over this place again and build Yourself another icicle in the winter. Who can comprehend Your greatness?"

Is God your traveling companion? Does He travel through each day with you? Are you like little six-year-old Andrew, saying, "Poppa, look over there!" Do you love to "direct" the gaze of God to the things you see? God loves to be directed this way, in the same way we love to share in the discoveries of our loved ones. Travel is fun when you are with someone.

But it's not just the good and beautiful things to which we call our Father's attention. He wants us to notice the hurts, pains, and difficulties too. As we say, "Father, look at this person's trouble or that corrupted mess!" He responds by casting His gaze upon that dark scene, and the light of His love shines in a special, warm way. When you see someone who is in obvious need, do you call the Father's attention to that person, quietly asking the Lord to notice and to help by shining His light and love? Do you have a "traveling" relationship with God so that each instance is seen in the light of His presence? Is prayer your "traveling companion" relationship with God?

Reflect/Discuss:
We have a tendency to confine prayer to a period of devotions. Describe some significant prayer experiences that have not taken place in a devotional time.

Meditate:
Prayer is a dependent, enfolded, empowering, "friend-in-the-middle," traveling relationship with God.

DAY 7

Prayer is work

Haddon Robinson first called my attention to prayer as work by asking the question, "Where did Jesus do the work of the atonement? In the garden, in the judgment hall, or on the cross?" Robinson said that in his estimation the real work of the atonement came when Christ sweat drops like blood, agonizing in prayer in the garden. Because Christ did the work of prayer, He could enter Pilate's judgment hall with quiet confidence, and on the cross He could say, "Father forgive them." However, because the disciples failed at the work of prayer in the garden, they deserted Jesus when He was arrested, leaving Him to face His trial and to hang alone on the cross. Prayer is our working relationship with God.

Every praying Christian must understand that his or her prayers are not simply "support" for various missions. They are the real work of missions. When done properly, they make it possible for the missionaries to perform the "mop up" operation! Wesley Duewel, a former missionary to India and a teacher of prayer, tells how his mission struggled for twenty-five years as it planted one new church a year. The missionaries decided that something was wrong, so they enlisted a thousand people in their sending countries to pray daily. In the next few years the mission exploded from 25 to more than 550 churches and from 2,000 to nearly 75,000 believers.

God intended for prayer to be the means by which we join with Him in His work of redeeming the world. When He invited us to "ask and receive," He was not implying that He would "do it anyway" if we did not ask. One of the most damaging beliefs the Devil plants in our minds is that prayer does not matter, as though God will do what He wants to do, whether or not we pray. In a broad sense that is true, for we know that God created everything without us and saved us without any help from us, for we were totally unable to help. But now that we are saved, He chooses to work through us. And there is a whole world out there in which we can say with confidence that God will not act unless we pray! Why else would God say to the Son, "Ask of me, and I will make the nations your inheritance" (Ps. 2:8)? Is God lying when He tells us that the primary method of delivering the nations to the Son is through prayer?

I think of prayer as a spotlight. When I pray for a specific area, I am calling God's attention to that target, focusing His spotlight on that area in a special way, illuminating places of spiritual darkness and death. When I go prayer walking, interceding quietly for each house I pass, I focus the light of God's love on that home, and I believe this is an extremely significant act. Something happens in that home—even though I may not see it—when I focus the light of God's love even momentarily on a house by praying for its occupants. I call God's attention to those people in a way that He would not attend if I had not prayed for them.

I also think of prayer as a sprinkler. Not only does the spotlight of God's love shine on a house, neighborhood, or nation when I focus my prayers there, but the shower of God's blessing falls with new, spiritual life. When I pray, I often think that in one hand I hold a spotlight and in the other hand I hold a hose and sprinkler. When I shine God's light on an area by praying for it, I also hold a hose on that lifeless place, watering it with God's blessings. Both things happen when we pray for a specific person or area—God's light of love shines, and God's blessing falls on it.

The majority of Western Christians do not understand this "working relationship" with God through prayer. In our arrogance we think God needs our money, our five-year plans, and our organizational expertise. But this is *not* what God desires of us. He wants us to maintain a working, traveling relationship with Him. He wants us to pray constantly, asking Him to shine His light and to shower His life-giving blessings on specific people and areas that need to know Him.

Through prayer God is preparing us for life in His presence. He does not want us to remain "six-year-old Andrews" on His lap forever. God longs that we mature to that moment we are eternally enfolded into Him. We will rule the universe (see 2 Tim. 2:12), and the instrument of rule will be prayer, or communion with God. We are currently in the training program!

Reflect/Discuss:
Describe situations in your neighborhood, family, or workplace that need the spotlight of God's love and the shower of God's blessing through your prayers.

Meditate:
Prayer is a dependent, enfolding, empowering, "friend-in-the-middle," traveling, working relationship with God.

why
pray
first?

It takes two feet to walk

We've seen that prayer is not some alternative to our many humanistic programs—as if we could say, "If all else fails, pray." Prayer is a relationship with the Creator of the universe. We were made and redeemed for communion with Him through prayer. This relationship is unique to us. Neither animals nor angels can enjoy such intimacy with God. We need to approach this in a balanced way, however, for we do not want to draw the conclusion that all we need to do is pray and everything will happen! Nothing could be further from reality.

Prayer is part of the process of walking with God. One of the earliest references to walking with God is Genesis 5:22–24: "Enoch walked with God 300 years… Enoch walked with God; then he was no more, because God took him away." Enoch and

Elijah were the only human beings to escape death. Both were translated directly from earth to heaven (see 2 Kings 2). Both enjoyed intimacy with God, and obviously both were filled with the Holy Spirit.

What does it mean to walk with God as Enoch did? Think for a moment about walking. What happens if you try to use only your right foot while your left foot is planted firmly on the ground? You go around in circles, getting nowhere! The same thing happens if you try walking with your left foot, except that you go around in circles the other way. In order to get anywhere, you need to use both feet.

Prayer and *work* are two spiritual feet God has given us, and we need to use both of them.

On the one hand, Christians who pray without working may be so heavenly minded that they are no earthly good. In fact, being close to God in prayer always results in our receiving work to do. Through prayer we sense God's leading to serve Him in one way or another. *So if a Christian claims to pray but doesn't work, we know that one is a fraud!* We all know pious frauds who say, "I'll pray for you," but never do anything—and eventually you doubt that they prayed even a single prayer. But even if they pray, God won't work through them if they are unwilling to work as well as pray.

On the other hand some Christians are always working but have little time for prayer. A friend asked me why I wasted "all that good time" in a board meeting praying for our mission. "You have been called to work and do business," he said. "You accomplish nothing when you spend your time praying. God expects us to do something!"

Christians who are constantly working without praying have never experienced that glorious, many-faceted relationship with Jesus that we focused on in our first set of readings (Days 1–7). Further, they reduce Christianity to little more than human effort. Everything can be explained in their churches; there is no mystery about what is happening. They have no more supernatural power than can be found in the good works of the local Rotary club. This is not to demean Rotary clubs and other helpful organizations, but merely to point out that they are not the church. All the great work they do can be explained on the level of common sense and wonderful organization. They can do it all without prayer. They work.

The body of Christ is supposed to be a community of people who "walk" with God in a balanced spiritual life of *prayer* and *work*. Prayer always leads to work, and work always grows out of prayer. When the two are combined, inexplicable things happen! When prayer and work go together, the results exceed the plane of common sense. The church that prays and works lives on the plane of the supernatural.

The Western church may be compared to a little boy trying to fly a kite on a windless day. He runs furiously up and down the sidewalk, pulling his little kite behind him, and as long as he runs, the kite flies. The moment the little fellow stops, the kite plunges to the ground. His problem? The wind isn't blowing. The Western church, with its members burned out from endless programs, seminars, classes, committee meetings, planning sessions, and organizational flow charts, is much like that boy.

We are too often trying to carry the church and its programs by our own efforts. The wind of the Spirit is not blowing.

What the church desperately needs is a new wind of the Spirit; but when the Spirit comes, we must not stop working or consider our work less important. The Spirit fills our work and lifts it up, far beyond the world of human expectations and limitations, doing "immeasurably more than all we ask or imagine" (Eph. 3:20).

Reflect/Discuss: *Which tendency—work or prayer— more accurately marks your spiritual life and that of your church?*

Meditate:
*It takes two feet, **prayer** and **work**, to walk with God.*

Which foot first?

Jesus tells us the way to perfect rest is to be "yoked" to Him (see Matt. 11:28–30). That statement seems contradictory to me. Bearing a yoke is hardly a symbol of rest. Oxen, yoked together, are not put in that position to sleep! We yoke animals to put them to work. Why, then, does Jesus say, "Come to me, all you who are weary and burdened, and I will give you rest. Take my *yoke* upon you and learn from me, for I am gentle and humble in heart, and you will find rest for your souls. For my *yoke* is easy and my burden is light"?

I think Jesus is talking to that little boy we mentioned in the previous reading (Day 8) who was running furiously up and down the sidewalk, trying to fly a kite without any wind. He is burning himself out running, and his kite is not flying. He is not "yoked" to Jesus, for if he were, the divine wind would be blowing, and he would only have to raise the kite into the air for it to take off.

One of the major false impressions of Christianity is that we are saved to experience "idle" rest. But Jesus does not save us to take an eternal nap; He saves us to be eternally productive. We become weary and burned out in doing good things for Jesus through our own efforts. We run and run, but nothing seems to take off, and all appears wearisome and heavy. The church leaves a wide wake of burned-out workers. It's not that the work is wrong, but without divine energy we quickly are consumed by all the work to be done. Jesus is saying that the cure for our weariness is to be yoked to Him.

We are no longer an agricultural people, so the image of a yoke means little to most of us. If we change the illustration to a more familiar one, maybe we can see better what Jesus is saying. Think of a Marine parade, in which everyone is in step and the whole company moves smoothly as one body. Or imagine a military funeral with six marines in full-dress uniform carrying a casket; the timing of their movements is incredibly exact. They move together as one. This is what being yoked to Jesus means. It means walking in step with Him. What would it look like if, in the middle of that military parade, one marine fell out of step with all the others? He would stand out, to say the least! What would happen if just one of those six marines bearing a casket was out of step with the other five? He'd tip the casket and cause the others to stumble! Farmers have told me that if two horses yoked together do not move in step, they really make no progress at all. Jesus is telling us that in order to have rest in our work, in order to gracefully produce fruit for Him, we must be in step with Him spiritually.

So it becomes a serious matter to determine which foot goes first. Do we work first and ask God to bless our efforts? Or do we pray first and ask God to show us how to work? How did Jesus start? He started with prayer.

Being idle is not the great problem of the Western church. Many evangelical churches resemble frenzied beehives of activity! They overflow with programs. Yet, we accomplish very little because we are out of step with Jesus. We often run the church like a corporation, with planning meetings, goals, and objectives; and when we have it all figured out, we bless it with a "word of prayer," asking God to give us success so that the world might know how smart we are.

I realize I'm being a bit sarcastic. But it is true that we rely far more on our efforts than on prayer. Because of our sinful nature, we put the foot of work before the foot of prayer. Each time we do that, however, we should remember the picture of the military parade in which one soldier is out of step with the others. When we start walking *in step* with Jesus, we start with the foot of prayer, not on the foot of work and human plans. When we start with prayer, we find rest and joy. A backward glance will make us laugh as we wonder in amazement at the unbelievable, humorous, and unexpected ways God uses us when we walk in step with Him (see Gal. 5:25). Things happen that defy our planning, show-ing that God is in control. And we rest—we relax as we, in prayer, snuggle into God's lap with His arms around us. When we pray, He drives us in His great tractor around His magnificent farm.

Reflect/Discuss:
Are you "in step" with Jesus—praying first and then working? Give illustrations.

Meditate:
To walk with Jesus you must start on the foot of prayer.

80 and 80

I suppose it could happen only in North America. In this part of the world pragmatism is so entrenched that Christians run prayer "experiments." We put our trust only in methods that "work."

A church decided to see how important it was to pray *before* contacting neighbors. They selected, at random, a neighborhood of 160 houses near the church. They divided the area into two sections and asked the congregation to pray intensively for one section of 80 houses. But prayer was not a high priority for the other section of 80 houses. After a period of prayer, the church planned to contact all the houses in the neighborhood. The church secretary would ask the people in the neighborhood if they had any prayer needs and would like to have someone from the church call on them to discuss those needs.

After the set period of prayer, the church secretary contacted all 160 homes, asking the same question and using the same approach. By phone she told them who she was, explained that the church was willing to include all who lived in the neighborhood in their prayer program, and asked if they had any specific prayer requests for which the church could intercede. She also offered to have a couple call if the neighbors had matters they would like to talk about for prayer. When she called the 80 homes that had not been prayed for, she found that only one person responded with a prayer request. But when she called the 80 homes that had been deliberately prayed for, she found to her amazement that 67 of these families responded with prayer requests, and more than 40 of them asked for visits from the church!

This is what Jesus had in mind when He spoke about "rest." When we are yoked to Jesus and we begin on the foot He begins with—that is, prayer—our task is lifted up in the wind of the Spirit and supernaturally sails along.

I learned this lesson in a unique way in my work for Mission India. While attending a prayer seminar, I was challenged to choose, if I were a pastor, between hiring a full-time director of music or a full-time "pray-er" for the church. It took me only a moment to decide that I wanted the "professional" intercessor. I got so excited about the idea that I challenged the board of Mission India to change the job description of one of our staff members to be exactly that. When the board balked, I threw out a "sign." If God would bless this strategy so that income would go up beyond anything we would have expected from hiring a fund-raiser in the coming year, we would know that this was God's will!

The board went along with the challenge, and Mission India hired a full-time, professional intercessor. This person in turn started our India Intercessor program, now with several thousand households praying for India every day. In the first year of this new prayer ministry the mission grew substantially, far beyond what any one fund-raiser could have been expected to do! And God has been opening unexpected doors ever since.[1]

I shared this story with a friend in India, who then told me that God had led him to do much the same thing in the same year—1992. He had labored with his little mission in a city in the heart of India for about ten years, and fewer than twenty little house churches had started. He and his wife were burned out and tired. He then decided to hire "professional" intercessors and to begin his mission work in prayer, not with human effort. A few years later he had twenty-two people reporting for prayer work every day! And the mission exploded to more than 160 little house churches in those few years.

Are you being "carried" along by Jesus on the wind of the Holy Spirit, or are you trying to carry Jesus along? It may be so simple a matter as being out of step with the Savior. To be *yoked* is to be *in step*—and when that happens, we find that the task is easy and light, for He is pulling with us. When prayer is first and work is second, we are in step with Jesus. With the work arising out of prayer, we shift from working in human power to working in divine power.

Are you attempting to run your spiritual life on a human power base, starting with human effort and planning and then trying to bless your efforts with a "word of prayer"?

Reflect/Discuss:
What would your reaction be if your church proposed to hire professional intercessors?

Meditate:
The most important step is the first step—the step of prayer.

DAY 11

Who is first–
He or I?

They asked me to be their church growth consultant. As pastors of a large suburban church, they had recently returned from a church growth seminar and had designed an exceptional organizational plan for their church. They thought I could help them implement it and asked if I'd be interested in a one-year contract.

I listened to the three pastors for longer than two and a half hours as they explained the organizational plan. When they completed the presentation, the walls were covered with flowcharts and boxes. I observed that the plan was very impressive, and I had no doubt they would fill their large auditorium several times each Sunday if they followed the plan carefully. "But," I said, "I don't see the gas tank!"

"What do you mean?" they asked.

"What makes this flow chart Christian? You could use the same thing to sell fast food or life insurance. I have listened to you for more than two hours, but I have not heard a word about prayer! Where does prayer fit in?"

They assured me they intended to "bathe" it all in prayer; and I responded skeptically: "That sounds like little more than good intentions. Unless prayer is at the center from which all of this flows, bathing it in prayer is little more than asking God to bless your program to show the world how smart you are."

I said I was not interested in helping to implement the organizational plan. I did, however, make a proposal. Since my devotional life was in pretty rough shape and I had no one to hold me account-able, I offered to meet with them monthly to pray for four hours.

One of the pastors got tears in his eyes as God convicted him. Quietly and firmly the three replied, "You have a deal." They volunteered to set aside the flowchart and let God have full reign in their lives.

What happened over the next four years is virtually impossible to chart, but we all agreed that if ever the truth of Ephesians 3:20 was illustrated, it was demonstrated both in our personal lives and in our ministries: "[God] is able to do immeasurably more than all we ask or imagine." We set aside our ministry and personal agendas and asked God to reach deep into our hearts and lead us into His ministry.

Within a month, one of the pastors accepted a call to the local Pregnancy Resource Center, and left the church. "What was this?" I thought. I wanted to show how marvelously God would work in that church, and the first thing He did was take a pastor away. The other two pastors stayed, but all four of us kept meeting for prayer, and God started His work deep in our lives. Various aspects of our marriages were touched and healed; our pasts were dealt with; our devotional lives were deepened. One pastor's teaching took on new perspective; the other pastor's stomach problems disappeared as he rejoiced in not having to carry God's load but just to be himself! The pregnancy resource ministry struggled awhile and then exploded nationally and internationally. God led Mission India into a whole new emphasis on prayer, out of which this book was born. The pastors' church grew to be far more vital than it could have been under a man-made growth plan.

All of this reminds me of what a pastor said to me after I gave a message on praying according the pattern of the Lord's Prayer. I stressed that we should start as Jesus does, praying first that God's name be hallowed and that people discover how great He is through His revealing names. The pastor remarked that, during the first year of his pastorate, his prayer life had been powerful but that, during the past nineteen years, it had been impotent. He decided, as he was listening, the difference was that during the first year he had prayed for God's name to be glorified, but in the past nineteen he had prayed that God would bless his programs.

Perhaps in no other age has marriage been under such attack as it is today. All our counseling seems to do little to stop the fighting and marital break-up so common both within and outside of the church.

A friend of mine counsels those who come to him wanting a divorce to spend as much time in prayer for the repair of marriage as they spent in fighting to destroy their marriage.

More than ever, we need to be praying for families—for our own and for others in the church. In praying for our homes we need to start where Christ started in the Lord's Prayer. We are constantly prone to pray for solutions to family problems, and that can seem so hopeless. But consider instead—we should lift our eyes to the Father and pray that His name be glorified, His kingdom come, and His will be done… in our families, in whatever way He sees fit.

Praying can become so dusty-dry and boring when all we do is concentrate on our problems. We must rather concentrate on God's name, kingdom, and will, affirming that He will work toward those great goals in all the family challenges we might face.

You'll be amazed at what will happen. God's will is going to be done, and hope will come.

Reflect/Discuss:

When is it wrong to pray for the success of a church or mission organization?

Meditate:

To begin with prayer means that our first longing is to hallow God's name and ask that His will be done.

DAY 12

Pray first—the Father commands it

I've made much of the fact that the first foot we use in walking with God is the foot of prayer. It's time now to look at this principle not merely from the view of reason but from the view of Scripture. Does the Bible have anything to say about our starting point in the Christian life? Yes!—and the proof that we should begin with prayer rather than planning lies in far more than proof texts. The proof is in the very example and words of the three Persons of the Trinity. God the Father *commanded* that we begin our mission activity in prayer. Jesus the Son *demonstrated* that the work of the atonement began in prayer. And the Holy Spirit *empowered* the early church because the believers prayed first. They did not devise a strategy to reach the world and then ask God to bless their plans.

God the Father commands us to begin in prayer. Speaking to the Son (and thus to us), He says, "Ask of me, and I will make the nations your inheritance, the ends of the earth your possession" (Ps. 2:8). Notice that this verse is both a command and a promise.

Psalm 2:8 says much about motivation for missions. Our basic drive to reach the world is not because humanity is lost, although it is. Our drive arises out of love for Jesus and out of the knowledge that the nations of the world are His, not Satan's. Because we love Jesus and we are His agents appointed to claim the world for Him, we ask the Father on His behalf for the nations of the world.

Moravian missionaries were among the most highly motivated and effective missionaries in church history. Their drive for missions lay in their exalted motivation: Worthy is the Lamb to receive His reward. These people were driven by the fact that Jesus, having gone through the agony of bearing our punishment for sin, was worthy of the reward of having all nations delivered to Him. This positive motivation of love, rather than human need, is what drove them.

But not only is the *motive* for missions that of looking to Jesus; the *method* of missions, too, is in looking to Jesus. We must look at divine methods, not at human ones. The primary way of reaching the world for Christ is by prayer—intensive, passionate, specifically directed prayer! We must pray for specific fields, specific people groups, and specific states and nations, asking the Father to deliver each one to the Son as His rightful inheritance for His redemptive work at Calvary.

Early in Israel's history, we find a picture of the relationship between prayers and those who are directly involved with God's mission work on the "front lines." The Amalekites attacked Israel soon after God delivered His people from slavery in Egypt (see Exod. 17:8–13). So Joshua and Moses formulated a plan. They selected some of the best men to go out and fight, probably in the best possible place with the best possible plan. At the same time Moses said he would stand "on top of the hill with the staff of God in [his] hands" (v. 9). Moses lifted his staff (a symbol of prayer), and as long as he kept it raised over the Israelite army, Joshua and the troops prevailed. But Moses was only human, so he grew tired—and whenever he let the staff down, the battle promptly shifted to the Amalekites' favor. So a stone was brought for Moses to sit on, and Aaron and Hur held up his hands until sunset. So Israel gained the victory.

Praying Christians take seriously the Father's command "Ask of me, and I will make the nations your inheritance." They know their work in God's cause is just as important as the work of those who are directly involved on the front lines.

Every Christian, in fact, is a full-time missionary! The work of missions is done at home by you who pray for missions regularly. Which of these types are you? Have you been called, like Moses, to raise the staff of prayer, or are you called, like Joshua, to be on the field of battle? The Father says we must *begin* by asking, and He will deliver the nations of the world to His Son. What a powerful statement of hope!

Reflect/Discuss:
Describe your "missionary" prayer life. What are the areas you are especially burdened to pray for, and how do you pray for them?

Meditate:
The first step in winning the world for Christ is prayer, not plans, for the Father says, "Ask of me, and I will make the nations your inheritance."

DAY 13

The example of Christ

The importance of praying first, not planning first, is clear not only in the command of the Father about making the nations the inheritance of the Son (see Ps. 2:8) but also in the life of Jesus. We often think of prayer as a tool given to us weak sinners to "help us out." But any study of the life of Christ quickly reveals that this perfect and Spirit-filled Man lived in prayer. Every major event of His life followed a period of prayer.

The temptations. The direct, personal encounters between Satan and Jesus followed a forty-day fast (see Matt. 4:1–3). Why do we read that the Spirit led Jesus into the desert? The Spirit was filling Jesus with His divine presence (see Luke 4:1), preparing Him for the encounter. According to Luke, Jesus went directly from His baptism at the Jordan into the desert for a forty-day fast. Why was a fast necessary for someone who was perfect? Why did Jesus have to give up food in order to pray? These are mysterious questions with perhaps unknown answers, but there is one clear lesson here. Jesus, being truly human, had to *begin on the "foot" of prayer* in order to face the ordeal of meeting Satan head on—hence the fast in the wilderness. As perfect as He was, His human nature demanded that He prepare not by planning but by prayer. This encounter must have taken infinitely more effort, more strength, more energy than we can imagine, for it so exhausted the Lord Matthew makes a point of stating that "angels came and attended him" (4:11). It was not incidental that Jesus prepared through prayer; He began His warfare with the Devil in prayer, and by doing so showed that He willingly lived in complete dependence on the Father.

The disciples. "Jesus went out to a mountainside to pray, and spent the night praying to God. When morning came, he called his disciples to him and chose twelve of them, whom he also designated apostles" (Luke 6:12–13). Our normal reaction to this event is to ask ourselves that if Jesus was perfect and sinless, why did He have to pray before choosing the disciples? Did He not already know the Father's will? If He could tell who people were before meeting them (see John 1:47–51), and could know what they were thinking without their disclosing their thoughts (see Luke 9:47), why did He have to spend all this time praying before selecting His disciples? We might also wonder why the selection was not 100 percent effective, for among the Twelve was one who betrayed Him. From a human perspective, the choosing of these disciples makes little sense. The only one among them who would pass a modern sales and leadership test would be Judas. The pattern Christ used in selecting the disciples is a definitive pattern for our Christian life; Jesus did not plan, consider qualifications, and set goals. He prayed! And out of that night of prayer the work of selection arose, divinely guided by the Spirit of God. Jesus did not ask the Father to bless His plans; rather, He asked the Father to reveal His (the Father's) plans concerning the disciples. Here, at this point, that seems so insignificant to us, is where the division comes between corporate structures and the church. One starts in human effort; the other is born of the Divine Presence, which comes only as we open our hearts in prayer. Jesus Himself, the perfect human being, showed us where we are to start!

His passion and death. Most significant of all is the fact that Christ began the final phase of His atoning work on His knees, in prayer, in the garden. This was no easy effort, and we should never think of prayer as easy. A case can be made for the observation that much of the agony of bearing our sins was suffered by our Lord not so much on the cross or in the trial, as when He sweat drops like blood, bringing His human nature into the perfect will of the Father. It was in those moments of strengthening His profound "enfolding" with the Father and the "indwelling" of the Spirit that the true battle over the Devil was won, for Jesus was able with serene calmness (rest) to stand before Pilate and to pray for the forgiveness of those who nailed Him to the cross. The disciples, in contrast, began this period in human effort, sleeping through the time of prayer and deserting the Savior to face the trial and the cross on His own.

Reflect/Discuss:

Give examples of the consequences of failing to pray first and simply plunging into a task with human plans and efforts. Are the consequences of this pattern of activity always bad?

Meditate:

Jesus began all major phases of His life not in planning but in prayer.

DAY 14

The example of the early church

I have a bit of the "salesman" in me, so it always hurts to read the story of the ascension in Acts 1. It hurts because, from all sales perspectives, Jesus missed a golden opportunity—the disciples were at an emotional high point. After the crucifixion, they had never been lower, wondering what happened to the One they believed to be the Messiah. How their spirits soared as the resurrected Jesus appeared to them for a forty-day period! During that time Jesus proved beyond any shadow of doubt that He was living and real. All of that climaxed on the glorious day of the ascension, as His followers watched Him rise until He was hidden from their sight by a cloud. Then two angels explained that Jesus would come again, in the same way they saw Him go. What a perfect moment to send someone out! What motivation to go into all the world and tell everyone of these marvelous things!

But instead of "hitting it" and getting on with the work at this high moment, the apostles did something that all of us would find frustrating. They did what Jesus had asked them to do—they went back to Jerusalem and *waited*—waited for the promised Holy Spirit. None of the gospel writers tell of their emotions, choosing only to record their obedience. But these disciples were sinful human beings, and I am certain they must have wondered why, after all these amazing events, they could not get started right away. Why wait? I can imagine Peter and a few of the other leaders longing to get going NOW!

But wait they did—in a ten-day prayer meeting in an upper room. During this time they replaced Judas with Matthias as the twelfth apostle, in an event that is merely recorded in Acts but never referred to again—and seemed to have little consequence. Far more important, though, is the fact that they prayed: "They all joined together constantly in prayer" (Acts 1:14). They were turning the keys in the gates of heaven and in the gates of hell.

In prayer, the disciples turned a key in the gates of heaven, and the Holy Spirit was poured out upon them. The Spirit did all that was promised. He empowered Jesus' followers with the resources of divine power and divine transformation, changing a bunch of cowards into fearless witnesses to the truth. This ragtag bunch of poor fishermen and farmers who, like their Leader, had little earthly wealth, were recipients of the wealth of heaven, and out of them came a movement that swept the world. Today this movement embraces one out of every seven people as a true believer—and one out of every three is a nominal follower! Wonders flowed from the Spirit's activity through the disciples. Miracles testified that this little band did not operate on the level of common sense and planning but on a plane of life that could only be described as supernatural. The wisdom of the Spirit, who searches the mind of the Father, was theirs as they opened the gates of heaven by being enfolded into the triune God in prayer.

How easy it can be if only we use the *key*! This is what Jesus meant when He called us to get in step with Him. To start our ministry at any other point means we limit ourselves to human effort. One of the great slogans of the success seminars of the New Age movement is, "What the mind can conceive, man can achieve." Although it's meant to be freeing, I find this statement incredibly boring compared to Paul's motto: "[God] is able to do immeasurably more than all we ask or imagine" (Eph. 3:20). Why would I ever want to limit my life to my feeble imagination when, if I start with prayer, I can unlock a life far beyond anything I could ever imagine?

On a more somber note, prayer is also the key that unlocks the gates of Satan's resistance to the spread of the Gospel. How long would the disciples have worked on their own, to gain 3,000 converts, as they did that first day (see Acts 2:41)? In response to their prayers, God, the Supreme Commander in the spiritual war of the cosmos, sent His angelic warriors to break down the gates of hell and push back demonic forces so the Gospel could pour in (see Matt. 16:18). The work of a praying Christian is to turn the keys in the gates of heaven and hell by praying. Every time you think prayer is not significant, just think of being locked outside your house or car on a winter day without the keys! You'd be left out in the cold without those keys. Prayer is the key to divine power that lifts us up and breaks down demonic resistance.

Reflect/Discuss:
Think of an experience in which God supplied resources beyond human expectation, in response to prayer. Tell someone about it today.

Meditate:
Prayer is the key that unlocks the resources of heaven and the resistance of hell.

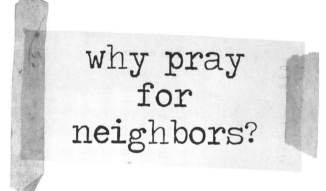

why pray
for
neighbors?

The foolishness of "pluck and plop" evangelism

Have you heard of "pluck and plop" evangelism? It's the most common form of evangelism practiced in the West. It's also the main reason not a single county in America showed a net increase in Christians in the past thirty years—despite all our "frantic" attempts to share the Gospel. We practice "pluck and plop" evangelism instead of "flip and flow." We concentrate on winning individuals to Christ, attempting to pluck them out of their natural neighborhoods and to plop them into our "mission compound," thus sterilizing them.

A good example of this method is found in an old book by J. Wascom Picket: *Mass Movements in India*. A mission labored for thirty years in India at

the close of the nineteenth century, with only five
converts to show for all its efforts. At the end of
this period, God used one of those converts to lead
Mr. Ditt, a tribesman, to Christ. Mr. Ditt, who was
in what used to be called the "untouchable" caste,
tanned hides for a living. He was illiterate, but when
missionaries brought him to the mission compound
and questioned him, they found he knew enough
about the Gospel to be baptized into the Christian
church—something that he deeply desired. After
the baptism the missionaries insisted that he remain
on the compound, for his tribe would persecute him
and perhaps kill him. They also wanted to offer him
more training in the Christian faith.

But providentially Mr. Ditt refused to stay on the
compound. Instead, he returned to his family. His
antagonistic brothers found out about his conversion and nearly killed him. But Mr. Ditt persisted—
and a few months after his baptism he showed up
at the mission compound with his wife and daugh-
ters, asking that they be baptized. The missionaries
were amazed that an illiterate man who had no

catechism training could so well prepare someone else for baptism, and they gladly baptized his family. They again invited Mr. Ditt to remain, but he insisted on returning home. A few months later he returned again, bringing his brothers for baptism.

In the next thirty years Mr. Ditt helped to win 300,000 of his tribe's people to Christ, while the mission sat on its compound, insisting on "pluck and plop" evangelism! The missionaries could not get beyond the concept of "winning individuals to Christ one at a time." They did not understand that God has placed us in neighborhoods. They did not understand that when Christ sent out seventy-two disciples to spread the Gospel by finding persons of peace in each village (see Luke 10), He was telling them to reach neighborhoods by winning individuals and not removing them from their surroundings. The disciples were to see those individuals as doors to the homes that should be "flipped" open so that the Gospel could "flow" in.

People are not merely isolated individuals to be won to Christ one at a time. A person is always part of a social fabric. A person has a home, relatives, friends, and neighbors, all who influence each other. When we pray for people we should always be praying for their home, their family, and their sphere of influence. In India new converts often want to immediately turn their homes into homes of prayer every day. We too must think beyond individuals, making certain that when they do come to Christ we do not "tear them out of their sphere of influence!"

Every Christian should be praying for three kinds of homes: Jerusalem homes, Samaria homes, and worldwide homes (see Acts 1:8). Jerusalem homes are the ones we live in. They consist of people we meet with regularly—next-door neighbors, friends, coworkers, and people at church. Samaria homes are the ones nearby, with which we seldom have contact. These may be suburbia or the inner city. Worldwide homes are all the other places and peoples.

Families are God's natural channels of communication. When one person, especially a child, becomes a disciple of Jesus, the entire home is blessed. The primary method of winning adults to Christ is to have their little ones lead them! As parents see the transformation of their children, they are opened to hearing about Christ in the most powerful way possible.

Reflect/Discuss:
Describe the neighborhoods you move around in. Have you ever thought of praying for them as a whole, or are your prayers limited only to individuals within them? Why would you want to pray for a whole neighborhood?

Meditate:
Don't use "pluck and plop" evangelism—use "flip and flow"!

Shining the spotlight of God's love in the darkness

Praying believers need to take the first step in transforming a neighborhood. If a neighborhood is to be changed, one or more Christians must target neighboring families in their daily prayers. A good way to ensure that every need of every home is prayed for is to follow the pattern of the Lord's Prayer, praying a petition a day and creatively applying it to the homes for which you are praying.

When a Christian or a network of Christians agrees to target specific homes in prayer, the spotlight of God's love begins to shine on those families. Think of the cluster of people, your target homes, as living in great darkness (see Isa. 60:2). Then think of one or two Christians praying for that target group. Those Christians become like the rising sun as its first rays creep out to chase away the shades of night. Or think of another analogy: the love of God shines in a home like the circle of light thrown by a theater spotlight upon the stage.

And when the light of God comes, inexplicable things happen. I think of the unexpected results when I organized six churches in suburban Chicago to pray for the inner-city housing development called the Robert Taylor homes. During a month of intensive prayer, those church members wrote to every apartment, offering a free Bible course and telling the residents that the church members would pray during that month for the complex. The complex became strangely quiet, and police calls dropped dramatically as the light of God shone on this dark, dark area! The mission reported that it was the quietest month in the recent history of the complex. What a tragedy that I did not know then what I know now—that God was leading us on to open up the Robert Taylor homes to the Gospel by forming prayer teams that would target these apartments. In traditional "planning" before "praying," we had decided that this would be a one-month attempt to get people enrolled in Bible courses, and we did not realize what transformation God worked through our prayers. We stopped praying, and the complex reverted back to darkness.

A couple that attended one of our seminars on prayer reported that God had led them to a strange experiment. They selected a shopping mall as their target area for prayer, and every Wednesday night they slowly walked through this mall, pausing briefly and as inconspicuously as possible in front of each store to ask God to shine the light of His blessing on it. They told me that after a few months the teens that hung out in the mall approached them and said, "We know what you are doing! But we have beaten you to it, for we have already prayed to Satan that he would curse each store!"

The couple continued to pray in spite of this strange threat. They prayed through the Christmas rush. Storekeepers and security guards caught on to what they were doing and expressed appreciation. And when the Christmas rush was over, they received some startling news. The mall had had the reputation of being the most violent in the city, with the highest incidence of police calls and shoplifting. That Christmas season, however, the mall came out on top as the quietest, with the least disturbance and the least amount of shoplifting. Storekeepers and guards could not help being impressed with this dramatic result to prayer, and those who were not Christians were curious about it.

I have often wondered what would happen if we targeted specific, troubled neighborhoods and saturated them in prayer, asking God to make His light shine. Is something like this not worthy of our effort?

Reflect/Discuss:
Describe some of the "neighborhoods" you know of. Describe their "value systems," contrasting a neighborhood that's open to Christianity with one that's closed.

Meditate:

*What are some of the "homes" in your life that need to be targeted in prayer **immediately**?*

DAY 17
Praise is the doorway into prayer

I tend to think visually. Most people do. Praying for a specific home is something like directing a spotlight on a group of actors in a play. The glow of the light encircles them in a bright round spot on the floor. When I pray for a specific home, I direct God's spotlight on that place. I am the stagehand working behind the scenes, asking God to shine His light on the specific area His Spirit has called me to pray for.

There's a special way in which this is done, however. It can only be done as I enter prayer through the doorway of praise. Charles H. Spurgeon said that praise is the doorway to prayer and that one ought never attempt to pray without going through that door. The Lord teaches us this truth in the outline He gives us in the Lord's Prayer. We are to begin with praise, as implied in the first statement, "Our Father in heaven" (Matt. 6:9).

Good conversation depends on how you enter into it. If you see someone you don't want to talk to, chances are pretty good that not much conversation will follow. But if you see someone you appreciate and respect, your expectations of a good conversation will often produce that very result.

Expectations in prayer are as important as expectations in conversation. If you plunge into prayer with petitions, and those requests usually are only centered in concerns for daily bread, your prayer life is likely to be extremely difficult and boring. You do not take time to enjoy God; nor do you have much faith in expecting results from your prayers. Often we leave prayer as heavy hearted as when we began, for we really do not believe that God is our Father in heaven whose kingdom is coming—even now! We don't expect much when we enter, so we don't expect much when we leave.

Thank God that both the Savior and the Spirit make constant intercession for us and correct our limited prayers (see Rom. 8:26, 34). But that is no excuse for insulting God with a lack of anticipation when we enter into prayer with Him. As you pray for a specific home, think of shining the spotlight of the love of the one, true, holy, magnificent God on it!

Every time you pray for that home, start by thanking God that He is the perfect Father and that the persons living in that home are His created image bearers. Thank God for the wonder of His creation in their lives, and praise Him for His goodness and gifts to each person in that area. Tear down the walls of doubt and despair that surround the home and set up walls of praise and anticipation at what God can and will do in it.

Do not interpret what is happening in terms of human comfort or happiness. Realize that as you pray, the heavenly Father has His own divine plan, which, in a very real way, is implemented as you pray. Remember that when the Father said, "Ask of me, and I will make the nations your inheritance"

(Ps. 2:8), He was also telling us that if we do not ask, those nations will not be given! Nations come to Christ one family at a time. Our prayers should always be for more than individuals. They should shine God's light on the entire sphere of influence of any person—their home, extended family, and friends. God indicates that nations can be brought to Him—it's there for the asking. We have every right to claim His implied promise.

As you begin your prayers, always think about God's greatness. Perhaps start with His greatness in creation and then move to His greatness as shown in redemption. Then think of God's greatness in defeating the powers of darkness in that home. Dream of what it will be like when God's name is hallowed and the Spirit's transformation comes (see 2 Cor. 3:18). Trust God that He will be faithful to His promise that when you ask Him for a people group, a nation, a home, with praise and confidence, He will transform it.

As you conclude your prayer for the home, reiterate the praise with which you began, focusing on

God the Father's glory and majesty and the coming of His kingdom in power here on earth as it is in heaven (see Matt. 6:9–10). As you think of that home, picture yourself as a stagehand shining God's spotlight on it.

Reflect/Discuss:
What homes will you pray for? What might they look like if the spotlight of God's love and praise were turned on them?

Meditate:
I should always begin my prayers with praise. Then, like a stagehand, I direct God's spotlight of love into a specific home.

DAY 18

Random acts of kindness

The light of God's love on a home is rather faint if all we do is pray. But when we allow God to use us as conduits through which His answers flow, the light of God is intensified. In India the evangelists we train always begin by forming a prayer team or network, saturating the target area with prayer. But then they also reach out in acts of caring.

Kali, the Hindu goddess of destruction, is worshiped in Calcutta and its surrounding areas. Kali is not pretty! She wears a necklace of decapitated human heads with blood dripping down her torso, and her skirt is composed of severed human arms. Tradition has it that Kali demands human sacrifice to appease her, and such sacrifices, even to this day, are not unheard of throughout the area. A Christian couple targeted several "Kali" villages north of

Calcutta and saturated them with their "remote" prayers. When they felt that God's Spirit had warmed a village and partially melted down the wall of hostility to Christianity, the couple moved in with a program that showed their love for children. Through a Children's Bible Club, they taught the children about Jesus for a two-week period. As a result, half of the children indicated that they wanted Jesus to be their God rather than the idols that their families served!

Selvi, a little twelve-year-old girl, was one of those whose lives were touched by Jesus, even though her parents were very strong in their devotion to Kali. Shortly after her decision to follow Jesus, Selvi's little sister became ill with a rare blood disease. She was taken to the local hospital, where doctors told the family she had only seventy-two hours to live. Selvi pleaded with her parents to allow the two Bible school teachers to come to the hospital to pray that Jesus would heal her sister. The desperate parents agreed. The teachers knelt beside the dying girl's bed and pleaded with Christ to spare her life for the sake of the Father's glory.

Twenty-four hours later the little sister walked home, completely healed. Selvi's parents and her grandmother who lived with her knew that Jesus was the real God, and they publicly smashed the stone idols of Kali in front of their house! Their home became a *new home of prayer every day*. This family, which had been touched by the specific prayers and concern of the Christians, began now to pray for their neighbors. Light came into their lives not only because a "remote" group of Christians prayed for the village, but also because the teachers showed acts of care and love by teaching their daughter and later praying for her in the hospital.

In his book *Conspiracy of Kindness*, Steve Sjogren tells of the random acts of love and kindness that members of his church do in order to give shape to the love of Christ in their lives. These acts of love range from handing out free soft drinks in Jesus' name at sporting events, to cleaning toilets in shopping malls, to washing neighbors' cars and raking their leaves.

In response to a message about prayer, a Christian named Jane decided to pray for three neighbors, starting in August. In September, on a strange "whim" she bought three Christmas wreaths at a craft store and put them in a closet in her home, not understanding why she did this. She continued to pray for her neighbors but never contacted them, so she did not know what was happening in their lives. At Christmas, she realized that God's Spirit had prompted her to buy the wreaths— she would give them to the three neighbors and tell them she had been praying for them, thus establishing contact. She took her six-year-old son with her as she called on these neighbors and informed them that she had been praying for them.

At the third home something strange happened. The woman who opened the door looked like "death warmed over." She appeared frail and sickly. Jane was so startled that she merely wished the woman a merry Christmas and gave her the wreath. As she turned to leave, her son said, "Mom, aren't you going to tell her you've been praying for her?"

The neighbor swung the door open again and said, "What did you say? Are you the one who has been praying for me the past few months? I've been so sick that I nearly died, and I felt the only reason I was alive was because someone must have been praying for me. I've been asking God to bring that person here. Are you the one?" Needless to say, a marvelous spiritual discussion followed as Jane witnessed to this neighbor for whom she had been praying but whom she had never met.

Reflect/Discuss:
What deeds of love and kindness would gain the most attention in your targeted prayer area?

Meditate:
Praying must be expressed in caring.

DAY 19

Praying, caring, and sharing

When we make our home a home of prayer every day by praying for other homes, geographic and cultural boundaries suddenly disappear. While we may not be willing or able to enter some areas of our city physically, we can enter them spiritually as we pray for the families living there. Prayer knows no boundaries. Through it we can lift up homes in any area.

Boundaries between communities in India are very high. The following story shows how families in one community transcended these boundaries through prayer.

Rural India is divided by caste. The caste system groups all members of Indian society into varying levels of privilege. There are four major castes, and if you are not born in one of them (because the Hindu gods are punishing you), you are born "casteless" or as an "out-caste." Even though the caste system is outlawed, it still exists and is very strong. High-caste Brahmins do not enter out-caste homes or associate with tribal people (who also are out-castes) in any social way. They do not eat together or even drink from the same well.

In one tribal out-caste village, many families became Christians, and they became concerned for the salvation of the high-caste Brahmins living on the other side of the river. They knew that the Brahmins would not talk to them, and so the families began to pray.

Stephen was a wealthy Brahmin living on the other side of the river. His wife had been ill for twenty years, and they had traveled far and wide to witch doctors and medical doctors seeking help for her. In spite of all their efforts and the money they spent, Stephen's wife remained seriously ill.

One night while Stephen and his wife were sitting on their veranda, they noticed a gathering of people in one of the huts of the tribal "untouchables" who lived across the river. Soon, singing came out of the thatched-roof building. This went on for several hours and continued several nights in a row. One evening Stephen's wife told him she had heard there were many miracles happening in the village as a result of these gatherings. She suggested that he go and stand by the river, facing the hut of the untouchables, to pray to this "new" God for healing.

At first he objected, reminding her that no self-respecting Brahmin would pray to the God of the untouchables. But she prevailed and he went, asking this unknown God to reveal Himself by healing his wife. If that would happen, he said, they would serve Him forever. He returned to his home, and to his amazement he found his wife totally healed. In great excitement they rushed over the bridge and did what no self-respecting Brahmins would ever do—they entered the home of the untouchables and demanded to know who this God was to whom they had prayed.

The untouchables told them about Jesus. They explained the way of salvation, and at that moment

Stephen and his wife became followers of the Lord as the Spirit gave them new life.

But there is much more to the story! The untouchables also told them they had been targeting the Brahmin community with their prayers, pleading with God to raise up workers to go into the Brahmin village because no one would ever listen to an untouchable, especially one who was telling them about a new religion. "You," they said, "are an answer to those prayers. God is telling you that you must go to proclaim the Good News to your own community." Stephen enrolled in Mission India's church planter training program. When I met him two years later, I learned he had been used by God to form a church of more than 200 Brahmin converts! When we make our homes **H**omes **O**f **P**rayer **E**very day, we open our doors to homes everywhere.

Praying, caring, and sharing. These are the three beginning stages in the transformation of a home or target area.

Reflect/Discuss:

What are some culturally appropriate ways of sharing the Gospel in the homes you are praying for?

Meditate:

Homes are transformed when prayer is expressed in care, and that leads to sharing the Gospel.

Don't move around from house to house

When Christ sent out the seventy-two (see Luke 10:1–23) he gave specific instructions as to how they were to carry out their mission. The heart of their mission was to find a specific home in a village. Upon finding that home they were not to "move from house to house" (Luke 10:7); rather, they were to stay in that home. The owner of the home was to feed them and care for them. This person is often called a person of peace, and that home would become the "sanctuary" in which Christ dwelled and from which blessings would flow.

Christ was instructing the seventy-two disciples to make homes of prayer everywhere they went. Ministry in the town was to be conducted from that home of peace (or prayer). They were not to move around from home to home, but from the home of prayer they were to heal the sick and proclaim the coming of Christ's kingdom. Likewise, the ministry goal of Mission India is to assist the Indian church in making homes of prayer every day, in every village. It is from these homes of prayer that the Gospel flows.

A friend was visiting some Gypsy villages in India. These fascinating, colorful people—who may be relatives of Italian Gypsies, for they speak the same root language—have long been very resistant to the Gospel. The entire village had assembled to hear my friend speak. His first question caused a great deal of commotion: "Have any of you ever met Jesus Christ?"

A considerable discussion followed as the people talked this over. The chief finally answered, "You can see that your question was taken seriously, and we have discussed it among ourselves. Since none of us have ever heard of this Jesus, we conclude that Jesus Christ does not live in this village."

Isn't that an interesting way to put it? "Jesus Christ

does not live in this village." That's why many villages in India and many neighborhoods in the West are so dark. Have you ever asked yourself what it takes to get Jesus to move into a village or neighborhood? The answer is found in Matthew 18:20: "For where two or three come together in my name, there I am with them."

When two or three in a family come together for prayer they make their home into a sanctuary, a dwelling place for the Holy Spirit. Every village in India has a Hindu temple or Muslim mosque in it. The Indian believers think of these as sanctuaries—the places where their gods dwell. In the animistic villages these sanctuaries can be special places, or special objects such as a sacred rock or tree. The Indians believe that both blessings and curses flow from these sanctuaries.

God does not dwell in sanctuaries made with human hands, as Paul pointed out to the Athenians in Acts 17:24. God has His own sanctuaries of human hearts. We in the West tend to think of these sanctuaries as individuals, but Christ points out that "where two or three are gathered in my name, there I am with them." It is our families, or little groups of believers, that become the sanctuaries in which Christ dwells. This does not mean that Christ does not dwell in each believer's heart; it does mean, however, that when two or more believers (especially in a family) come together in worship and prayer, they bring to the community the presence of Christ in a special way.

A popular praise chorus begins with the words, "Make me a sanctuary..." That is a typical, individualistic, Western approach to Christianity. Christ desires even more—that we make *our homes* sanctuaries. When that happens, blessings of transformation flow from us into surrounding areas. The temples of Christ are foremost the Christian homes in which daily praise and prayer open the windows of heaven, showering down God's blessings on the entire area.

The Holy Spirit dwells in all believers, and when they pray in accord with the Spirit, great power is at work—power that is uniquely effective in those who have been made righteous through Christ (see James 5:16). So when God's people meet regularly in prayer for specific homes, the Spirit of Jesus is literally present and at work in that location. That's how a neighborhood is transformed—through the prayers of God's people who have the presence of the Holy Spirit.

One day we were racing through the countryside of the state of Andhra Pradesh in southern India when our Indian-evangelist driver slammed on the brakes, jumped out of the car, and opened the door for me to get out. "Remember this village?" he asked me excitedly.

"No," I said. "I haven't been here before."

"Yes, you have!" he said. "This is the village where after just three months we had twenty-five baptisms!"

"But," I said, after I looked around, "it looks so different. It's so clean. The people seem so happy."

"That's because Jesus lives here now!" the evangelist said. "We built a living home, made of living stones for Him, and that living home is a holy priesthood offering daily prayers for this village. And look at how the village has been transformed because Jesus has a sanctuary here." (See 1 Peter 2:5.)

Reflect/Discuss:
Make a list of the homes that your "home of prayer" will be praying for daily. Have each person contribute a personal list of homes for which he or she will pray daily. Share ways in which God is changing these homes and opening the door to transformation so that they will become homes of prayer every day.

Meditate:
Are you trusting that God will really transform the homes for which you pray?

By multiplication, not addition

It's amazing how we limit the spread of the Gospel by thinking of evangelism in terms of winning individuals to Christ rather than transforming homes. Jesus told us to make disciples, and they always come in pairs! There's no such thing as an "individual" disciple. It takes two to become a disciple. Read Christ's definition of discipleship found in John 13:34–35. He describes disciples as persons in a visible love relationship, with a love for each other so great that it defies explanation and is the ground by which non-Christians judge whether we are truly Jesus' disciples!

The book *Your Home, a Lighthouse* tells this story:

Shortly after Arlene became a Christian, she developed a concern for her family, who were of another faith. She drove two hours to her mother's home to tell her what had happened in her life, totally unprepared for her mother's response: "I can't believe you are turning your back on the way I have raised you." Crushed, Arlene cried all the way home.

She called to tell me what had happened. "Well, why don't we just pray about that?" I said. "You know, maybe you should start a Bible study at your sister's home. Do you think she would do that?"

Arlene said, "That's two hours away."

"Bob and I will go up once a month to lead the study, if your sister will host it," I told her.

Arlene's sister reluctantly agreed, and after about six months she received Christ. Then, in sequence, her husband, four children, and mother became Christians. Then Arlene's sister led her father to Christ.

Bob Jacks provides a chart or "map" of the various homes reached by Arlene and her Christian friend Bob. Six homes were touched by an evangelistic

Bible study and prayer cell. Within one year over 104 persons were transformed, and their homes were in turn transformed into homes of prayer. This, by the way, occurred in the state of Connecticut, which is not known to be the world's most responsive area.

When we were first experimenting with the formation of homes of prayer, we hired a church planter to start one "cold" on a street in the inner city. One Wednesday afternoon, after much prayer and guidance, he and his wife selected a street and went from door to door, asking neighbors what they thought the needs of the neighborhood were and if they would be willing to form a home of prayer. To the couple's delight, on that first afternoon someone was interested. This person had not been to church for thirty years but considered herself a Christian and felt the only solution to the neighborhood problems would be prayer. The church planter encouraged her to invite her neighbors to a meeting with him the following week.

A week later he was dumbfounded to find that fifteen people had shown up to pray for the neighborhood! After a prayer-and-worship time, a woman identified herself as a resident on "the next street over." She said she would like to start her own home of prayer for her street. So on the third week, there were two groups praying for their streets. Within a month, a third person, from the second group, asked if she could start another home of prayer. A policeman from a fourth street also asked for help in starting one on his street! Within a few weeks a mini-explosion occurred, as people's homes became homes of prayer.

No, God doesn't always work that way. I am now working with an inner-city apartment complex for which a home of prayer has been praying for two years! Crime has dropped dramatically, but we have not been able to start a home of prayer in any of the twenty buildings. Within two months of starting in another city housing project of 250 units, however, homes of prayer began emerging on every floor.

Reflect/Discuss:
Describe a situation in which you have seen the Gospel race from one home to another.

Meditate:
When you think of witnessing, never think merely of individuals. Think families, think homes. Make your goal that of Luke 10:7—find homes that will become homes of prayer in the area.

how should
we pray?

DAY 22

"Hallowed be Your name"

Every home has the same set of seven needs—the needs identified by Jesus in the structure of the Lord's Prayer. And just as Jesus taught His disciples this prayer when they asked, "Lord, teach us to pray …" (Luke 11:1), our Savior teaches us through the Lord's Prayer how to pray for our neighbors. (See Matt. 6:9–13.)

Every family needs to discover who God is by *hallowing His name*. In those homes *His kingdom must come* and *His will must be done*. Every home must learn to *depend on God for everything* and *turn to Him for forgiveness, or reconciliation*, before renewal can begin. Every home needs *God's leading away from temptation* and *His deliverance and protection from evil*.

I have often struggled in prayer with the simple question "What must I pray for?" I find that prayer lists and prayer requests are not only boring but often seem insulting to God. They seem so narrow, so trivial, and so often they are very self-centered. Nothing corrects this problem as quickly and simply as using the seven petitions of the Lord's Prayer as your prayer outline for each week, praying a petition each day.

Start where Jesus tells us to start, praying for the hallowing of God's name. To do that, we must know what the names of God stand for and what it means to "hallow" those names, or to lift them up as holy.

The names of God are descriptions of His character. When God calls Himself the Good Shepherd, for example, He is describing His nature as that of a self-sacrificing shepherd who lays down His life for His sheep (see John 10:11). To hallow the name *Shepherd* in a home means asking that the family—each individual in it—may have a special experience or discovery of the shepherd aspect of God. We ask that they may learn, deep in their hearts, what it means to be in God's flock.

You might pray like this: *Father, I adore You. I praise You that You created every person in this neighborhood and gave to each one Your image and likeness. I praise You for the wonder of Your work in creation. How tragic it is, Father, that families have no idea who You are. They do not know Your nature. They do not know Your glory or Your love. Savior, You are known for being our Shepherd. You describe Yourself as the Good Shepherd who lays down His life for His sheep. Today I plead, heavenly Father, that all in my home may discover and experience Your tender, Shepherd care. Somehow, some way, let them each know Your Shepherd love. Please, Father, do this for my family and these other families: [list their names and the specific reasons why they need to know God as a Shepherd].*

Make a list of all the common names of God, and creatively use them every Sunday, the first day of each week, as you pray for your family and other families. Here are just a few of the more common names of God found in the Bible:

Prince of Peace
Everlasting Father
Wonderful Counselor
Mighty God
Immanuel ("God with us")
Savior
Holy Spirit
Comforter
Healer
I AM WHO I AM
Jahweh, the God who keeps His promises
Provider
Creator
King of kings and Lord of lords

Reflect/Discuss:
What is your favorite name of God, and why?

Meditate:
Read Psalm 23 and think about what it means today that God is your Shepherd.

DAY 23

"Your kingdom come"

The Devil knows about kingdoms. I think of the Devil's words to Jesus in Luke 4:5–7: "The devil led him up to a high place and showed him in an instant all the kingdoms of the world. And he said to him, 'I will give you all their authority and splendor, for it has been given to me, and I can give it to anyone I want to. So if you worship me, it will all be yours.'" Jesus did not dispute the Devil's claim; He did not deny that the world's kingdoms belonged to Satan. The Devil led Adam and Eve into sin, and thereby became the prince of the kingdoms of this earth.

Is it any wonder that Jesus not only taught us to pray, "Your kingdom come," but also spoke frequently about the kingdom of His Father and its coming to earth? What greater need can there be than to

have the kingdom of God come to a home and re-
place the existing kingdom of darkness? I think of
an apartment complex near my home where, out
of fifty-four families, only two have fathers. The
government has become the father and husband
in those households; the government is their only
security. The kingdom of darkness rules in this complex; people are afraid of each other and will not
enter each other's homes. The area crawls with drug
dealers. Little children are not safe; they have no idea
what a protective, caring father is.

What would it be like if the kingdom of God
came into that complex? Imagine it for a moment.

First of all, people would be born again. Apart
from the Holy Spirit, change in a sinner's heart is
impossible. I sat next to a former crack addict at a
Bible study in the community room of that apartment complex, and I listened in awe to his testimony.
He told how he used to get high on crack—how it
tasted to him and what it did to him. "And then a few
years ago," he said, "I found Jesus, and He tasted so
good that at that moment my taste for crack disap-

peared." The kingdom of God had come into the man's heart as he was born again (see John 3:3). The Savior set up His throne in that person's life. When we pray for the coming of the kingdom, we plead with God for new life in the heart of each person in the home.

But the kingdom of God is so much more, for when it comes, God's light shines in the darkness. The little children in the complex would come to know what a father is, for the men would be born again and would come in faithfulness and commitment to the mother of their children and live in a wholesome, tender, providing relationship. My eyes fill with tears as I think of what these little ones miss because the kingdom of God has not come to their home. Their place is what the Devil spoke of when he offered Jesus the kingdoms of the world. But Jesus came so that the kingdom of darkness would be destroyed (see 1 John 3:8), along with all the evil that goes with it—the drug and alcohol abuse; the murder, rape, and other violence; the hatred, selfishness, and greed. Asking for the coming of God's kingdom is one of the most practical prayers you can pray.

Homes in darkness live by the satanic principle of *getting*. Everyone has one motive in life, and that is to *get* something for himself or herself without regard for others. When God's kingdom comes, the value of the family changes from *getting* to *giving*. *Giving* occurs within families and between families.

Here is a prayer you might pray: *Father, I long today for the coming of Your kingdom in my home and in [list the homes and families you are praying for]. I plead first that Your kingdom may come in the spiritual rebirth of faith in You alone. Through the presence of Your Spirit, I ask for this rebirth for [list the persons' names]. I also plead, Father, that You will take this home back from demonic control and establish Yourself as King. May every family member acknowledge You as King of kings and Lord of lords, not just with their mouths, but also with their lives. As King, make the families whole again, as You intend families to be in Your kingdom. Lord, I anticipate with joy and praise the inexplicable miracles You will do as Your kingdom comes. I tremble with anticipation as I praise You that Yours is the kingdom and the power and the glory forever!*

Reflect/Discuss:
What are some practical suggestions of ways to have God's kingdom come into our home?

Meditate:
What would my home be like if God's kingdom fully came to it?

DAY 24

"Your will be done on earth as it is in heaven"

The third great need in every home is *unity*. The wonder of God's kingdom is that it is a "one-willed" place; a place of divine harmony, for all are agreed on one will—God's will. Not only are all *agreed*, but they also *do* God's will. Doing God's will is active obedience.

As I target specific homes, and my own home, in prayer, I often use the Ten Commandments to pray for God's will to be done. Sometimes I pray all ten of the commandments (see Exod. 20:1–17). Sometimes I concentrate on the great summary of the law: that I must love God above all and my neighbor as myself (see Matt. 22:37–40).

One of the great needs in our homes is obedience to the first and second commandments—namely, that we worship God only and have no idols, making nothing in our lives more important than God. While the West may not consider itself idolatrous, the definition of idolatry given in Isaiah 2:8 shows that it is, for in this culture people worship "the work of their hands." I shall never forget when the Holy Spirit applied that teaching to my life as a born-again Christian and as a mission leader. I became convicted that the success of my organization had been more important to me than the glory of God's name, and thus I had turned the mission into an idol—the work of my hands. How easily we can do that. Virtually anything can become an idol.

Another form of idolatry is fear. When we fear something, we make it bigger than God in our minds. We say, "God, this is out of control. I worry because I think this threat is bigger than you can handle." The apostle Paul advises us in Philippians 4:7, however, that the peace of God will guard our hearts and minds. When our hearts and minds are fearful, we do not look at God and we have no peace. To pray for God's will to be done in a home is to pray that all forms of idolatry, especially pride and fear, will cease.

Pray that the language in your neighborhood homes may reflect honor and glory to God, and that His name not be dragged through the mud by constant swearing. Do you long for God's name to be honored? Does it bother you when you think that Jesus' name might be mentioned in neighboring homes only as a curse instead of a blessing?

Have you ever thought of praying for a day of rest for the homes that God has placed upon your heart—a special day set aside from the frantic pace of daily life, giving opportunity to reflect on God? Is it wrong to pray for the shutting down of offices, shops, and factories for one day a week so that we may be re-created in our worship of God? To pray for God's will to be done is to pray that the frantic pace come to a halt, that the never-ending pursuit of more and more money will end and we will have time to breathe spiritually and worship the Lord.

Then, as you pray, move on to relationships. Are

parents being honored? Is authority respected in your homes? Does God long for us to pray about this aspect of His will? Think of the hatred that exists in some families—and the actual abuse and murder spawned by it. One of the most powerful things we can pray for is the fulfilling of God's will in our families. Pray for the restoration of respect for parents and authority.

Pray also for God's will to be done in the way people treat each other. People are persons, not playthings. How many neighborhoods and families are shattered through lust, pornography, and adultery? God's people should be on their knees weeping in remorse and repentance over the daily TV shows that glamorize illicit sex and violence. Pray against the stealing and the lies that are so easily accepted as a part of modern life.

Then there is coveting, the fanning of greed and the desire to get. Coveting is pounded into us by every TV channel. Advertisements everywhere are designed to awaken coveting and desire, telling us the lie that we *need* the latest product and that life would be so much better if we had it. When you intercede for God's will to be done in your home and the other homes on your heart, you pray the teachings of the Ten Commandments, asking that your neighbors grow to love God with all their heart, soul, strength, and mind, and to love others as themselves.

Reflect/Discuss:
Which of the Ten Commandments is most flagrantly violated in your home? Why did you select this one? What will you pray as you ask for God's will to be done with respect to that commandment?

Meditate:
God's kingdom is a "one-willed," harmonious place in which all agree that God's will is the will to be done.

"Give us today our daily bread"

Sam was a chronic worrier. If he didn't have something to worry about, he would make something up. He always complained, and therefore being around him was an unpleasant experience. But one day, when Sam stopped at the local diner for his morning cup of coffee and donut, he was smiling and humming to himself. All the men in his coffee group were amazed at this sudden change, so they asked what had happened. Sam explained that he had hired someone to do his worrying for him, so he no longer had to worry and complain. The men were amazed and asked how much it cost to get someone to do that. Sam said it cost $1,000 a day! When they asked where he would get the money to pay this man, Sam replied, "I don't know, but I'm not going to worry about it. That's what I hired him to do!"

This fictional story has an element of truth in it, for the Christian has Someone to do all his or her worrying. One of the great honors we do God is to allow Him to worry about our troubles and thus free us to live in peace. Often, when I lie awake at night fretting about some problem, I'll pray, "God, there really isn't much sense in both of us being awake with this problem. So can You take over and worry about it for me?"

In teaching us to pray for our daily bread—that is, to ask for the things we need each day—Jesus indicates that He will do our worrying for us. He brought this home to me forcefully a few years ago in an interview with an Indian church planter who had graduated from our training program and had planted a little church in his fishing village. I called on him a year after graduation and asked how things were going. His was a most dismal story, for he told how all fifteen families who had been converted had reverted back to Hinduism. But to add to his woes, he had been expelled from the village and fined 6,500 rupees. Further, because his fishing boat had been confiscated, he had no means of feeding himself. I wept as I heard his story; and as I left, he asked if I could give him money for a new boat. As I reached into my pocket to take out my wallet, I heard these words come out of my mouth, "No, Peter, we don't give money for boats. But we will pray for you!"

At first, I didn't realize I had said that. But Peter evidently had more faith in praying for daily bread than I did, for he seemed delighted. As I walked out of that village, I felt I was the biggest hypocrite in India! I couldn't believe I had offered to pray for him, when I had enough money in my pocket for a little boat. I felt so guilty that, when I got back home, I asked many people to pray for Peter.

The following year God arranged for me to meet Peter again. When we met, Peter told me a most amazing story! The original fifteen families of converts had begun straggling back to the faith. But, what's more, Peter had planted nine more churches!

And, rather incidentally to Peter, God had given him enough money to get a new boat, and he was no longer banished from the village! A year later, he was even elected president of the village.

All this happened, I believe, because we prayed, "Give Peter his daily bread." And the Lord impressed on me that if I had merely given Peter money for a boat, without prayer, I would have crippled him for life. From that point on he would have depended on Western funds for the spread of the Gospel, not on the resources of Christ. Prayer had freed him to be what God wanted him to be and would equip him to be.

As Christians, our task is to pray for God's provision. He has the wealth to pay for the work of missions, and He will gladly release the resources needed to all who ask in faith. We often get sidetracked as we think of praying for the miracles of healing—are not experiences like Peter's also miracles that are just as God glorifying and wonderful? I think of Keith, a banker in my church who dotted every "i" and crossed every "t." He got so excited at a Faith Promise mission conference that he recklessly nearly doubled his usual gift. At home, that night, this man who always planned everything so carefully went into agony over how "foolish" he had been. The next day, however, a previous employer called, asking him to do a consulting task and offering him the *exact* amount that Keith had so "recklessly" pledged for missions the day before. This genuine miracle brought him to tears of joy and praise of God.

As you pray for the needs of your home, do so in joyful anticipation of God's miraculous provision.

Reflect/Discuss:
What are some experiences you have had in God's miraculous provision of daily needs?

Meditate:
"My God will meet all your needs according to his glorious riches in Christ Jesus" (Phil. 4:19)

DAY 26

"Forgive us... as we forgive..."

It's love that makes the world go round"—I think there's an old song that says something to that effect. Sandi Patti sings a song called, "Love in Any Language." Country and western, rock and jazz, golden oldies, classical, opera—in virtually every kind of music many of the songs focus on longing to love and be loved.

The fifth petition of the Lord's Prayer addresses this longing. The prayer for forgiveness is for reconciliation with God and with each other. In other words, it's a prayer for love. The entire purpose of the crucifixion can be summarized in Christ's first words from the cross: "Father, forgive them, for they do not know what they are doing" (Luke 23:34). He came to bring forgiveness.

Walk the streets of your neighborhoods and think of what goes on in the homes there. I think of one family, in which the husband, a veteran, has never recovered from the war in Vietnam. He struggles with alcohol and drugs. One night he shot up the house with a pistol. He has withdrawn from his family, caring little for them. The wife struggles along, bearing not only this burden and the task of raising three teenagers but also the daily hurts heaped on her by her so-called Christian parents, who refuse to talk to her and blame the whole situation on her. She becomes so depressed that she can hardly live another day. Somehow the lines to God need to be unblocked so that the Spirit can pour in with reconciliation not only between her husband and the Lord but also between the husband and his family, and between the wife's parents and the Lord. Only when the fullness of the Spirit comes and these parties experience the freedom of forgiveness will reconciliation flow. How many homes in your neighborhoods are war zones in which people are constantly at each other's throats?

An African-American friend of mine, a former professor at a state university, used his position to rail against all whites. He made an illegal mistake one day and was put into prison on drug charges. He became more bitter than ever. His wife divorced him, and his children left him. He swore he would never, ever deal with another white person.

Then God touched my friend's heart with forgiveness. With the help of a friend who could read, a blind white girl led him to the Lord. This young woman was teaching prisoners about Christ through Bible correspondence courses. God works in strange ways, and this amazingly gifted man ended up marrying this young woman. Now, together, they carry on a ministry of forgiveness and reconciliation in one of the toughest areas of the inner city. They live and move in the world in line with this petition: "Forgive us our sins as we forgive those who sin against us."

Seething anger within a man, unrecognized, boils out in abusive behavior toward his wife and children. He usually has no understanding of the turmoil within him that makes him lose control and hurt those whom he loves. But then God reaches into the man's heart and shows him what he is really like, breaking him into a thousand little pieces. He weeps, and in his utter futility, he reaches out to God. He is amazed at the love the Father lavishes on him, and in the freedom of forgiveness he finds himself transformed into a child of God (see 1 John 3:1). Uncharacteristic gentleness and concern supernaturally spring up in his life as a direct result of the Holy Spirit's living in his heart. Forgiveness flows from him, and he asks for forgiveness.

Talk about need! Is there any need in society today, in an average, ordinary home, like this need for forgiveness from God? As you pray for forgiveness and reconciliation in your neighborhoods, be specific in your requests. Plead with God that the grace of forgiveness may abound in specific ways to meet specific needs.

Reflect/Discuss:

Can you relate a positive story of someone whose life has been transformed through the experience of forgiveness and reconciliation with others?

Meditate:

"He himself is our peace, who has...destroyed the barrier, the dividing wall of hostility" (Eph. 2:14). That barrier is between God and all humankind.

"Lead us not into temptation"

Mary Gee, a missionary in India around 1950, worked in a village near Vellore for about eighteen months with little success. When Dr. Ira Scudder, a well-known missionary doctor, visited this village for a week many amazing things happened. When he left, the villagers asked Mary: "You have been here a year and a half, and yet very few things have happened. Far more happened while that man was here for a week than in all the time you have been with us. Does he serve a different god than you do?"

Deeply upset by this question, Mary visited Dr. Scudder and asked him what he had done. She was surprised by his answer: he had taught the villagers how to "listen" to God and be led by Him in prayer. He told them to isolate themselves, quiet themselves before God, and ask God to "turn off all bad ideas and thoughts in their minds." Then, in prayer, they could present to the Lord the problem that disturbed them. After asking God for leading, they were to wait and write down the first thoughts that came to mind and then go out and follow the instructions. Strange and beautiful things were happening throughout the village as a direct result of the people's prayers.

So Mary decided to try this rather unique approach to being led by God. She knew what she would pray for: she had been fighting with her neighbor, a widow with ten children. She and her neighbor simply could not get along. Mary prayed that God would lead her away from the temptation to continue to fight with her neighbor and to enable her to reconcile with the neighbor. Then she waited. The first idea that came to her was "Take her an egg." Mary wrote the words on a piece of paper, and then, in disgust, she wrinkled up the paper and threw it away. If that was how God was going to lead, she thought, she didn't want any part of it.

Mary went to school to teach for the morning. When she came home for lunch, she found a chicken in her kitchen chair. She shooed the chicken away, only to discover that the chicken had laid an egg on the chair! She was embarrassed. Evidently, God had done more than give her a thought to write down; He had given her the egg as well! So, with considerable reservation, Mary took the egg next door.

Instead of going into the house to face her neighbor, Mary gave the egg to her neighbor's youngest child, who was playing outdoors. She instructed him to take the egg to his mother.

The following noon, Mary's neighbor paid her a visit. "Why did you give me that egg yesterday?" she asked. Mary told her the entire story, confessing that she was trying to listen to God's leading but did not believe the answer was really from God, since it seemed so strange. After all, Mary thought, what good would one egg be to such large family? Then Mary's neighbor told her side of the story: She had given all the food in the house to her children and had nothing for herself to eat. She had been praying that morning, "Lord, if you could just get me one egg by noon, I'll be able to get through the day." She explained how surprised and delighted she was when her little boy brought the egg to her at noontime!

As the two shared their stories, God worked His amazing reconciliation. They agreed to stop fighting. Then they prayed together, asking God to bless them and make them the best of friends.

When we pray that God will lead us away from temptation and sin, we must know how to listen to God. If you do not like the method Mary learned from Dr. Scudder, then you must develop your own method. But whichever way you pray, you must know that an important part of prayer is learning how to listen as God speaks to you! He speaks by applying specific teachings in the Bible to specific needs and challenges in your life. He speaks through friends, through circumstances, through strange "coincidences." One of the greatest thrills in life is that of learning how to listen daily to God.

Use this day to learn how to listen to God, especially to learn what He wants you to do to express His love to your neighbors. Learn from Mary's story. Don't crush impulses to perform strange acts of love and kindness. They may be God's humorous and delightful way of using you in remarkable ways.

Reflect/Discuss:
Describe a time when you "heard" God lead you in some unusual way.

Meditate:
I must learn to listen to God.

"Deliver us from the Evil One"

Yes, Jesus teaches us to pray with regard to Satan, the evil one. We need to ask the Lord for deliverance from Satan and for protection from him. We need to learn about demonic influence not merely as it relates to individual people, but also as this influence affects entire homes.

Our work in India taught us that a person can be held in the control of evil forces, not merely because of opening himself or herself to the influence of the Devil but also because the entire home is under demonic control. When we pray for a specific home, we must always end the prayer as Jesus taught us—by praying that the area will be delivered and protected from the evil one.

I think of Goa, a popular tourist spot on the western coast of India. Settled by the Portuguese, its current religion is a strange mixture of Catholicism and Hinduism, and its one central characteristic is a hostility toward evangelical Christianity. An Indian pastor told me that he had often tried during a period of twenty years to plant house churches in that region, but never had much success. Only six or eight churches existed, and they were struggling.

A team of intercessors from Brazil went to Goa in the summer of 1995 and rented a house. Their sole intention was to pray for the city—and specifically that the horrible demonic hold on it be released. They spent an entire year in serious, heavy intercession for the deliverance of the city. At the end of the summer in 1996 they returned home. They had done no evangelism. Then my friend told me that in September and October, immediately after their departure, his ministry planted more than twenty new house churches! It seemed as if all the resistance had melted away.

Calcutta, a city named for and dedicated to the terrible Hindu goddess, Kali, has always been a place I dreaded visiting (see Day 18, "Random Acts of Kindness"). On my arrival in the airport I would often find myself falling into a strange depression. As I traveled the city streets, my mood usually grew darker. The city is so *full* of suffering. I would begin to feel that it was hopeless to work there. But I am not alone, for many of the Christian workers in this goddess-controlled city feel the same way. They, too, struggle with discouragement and depression.

In October 1996 I had an opportunity to visit Calcutta, and I had an entirely different experience. As I entered the airport, I felt that tons of spiritual heaviness had been lifted from my shoulders. My wife and I got into a taxi, and as we went down to central Calcutta, the taxi driver was playing Christian hymns. Instead of the usual gray, depressed feeling, I found my spirits bouncing as we began singing hymns. When we checked into our little hotel, I was informed that there were some other North Americans on the third floor who had recently checked in. I had met one of them years ago in Canada, and I wondered what they were doing there.

We eagerly went to their room, and then it dawned on us! This was the month in which millions of Christians were praying for major cities in the 10/40 window (degrees of latitude), and Calcutta was being prayed for *that very day!* The team of North Americans had come to Calcutta for a few weeks of on-location intercession for the city. Specifically, the team was pleading with God to deliver Calcutta from the control of demonic powers and protect it from future attack.

As I visited with our friend there, he related that a strange thing had happened to him the night before. He had a dream in which he saw the city of Calcutta as a sick man, lying in a hospital bed, wrapped in bandages from head to toe. A doctor came and started an IV on the man—and then Jesus appeared in the dream and asked my friend if he knew what this meant. He said that he did not. Jesus said, in this dream, that He had heard the prayers for Calcutta and had begun the process of healing this very sick city. In the following months tremendous new encouragement came to the workers in the city.

The Lord's Prayer is a most important guide in prayer for your own home and others! By praying it, crime can decrease in violent areas and beautiful miracles can occur. Ask God to bless your homes, delivering and protecting them from demonic influence.

Reflect/Discuss:
Describe a specific experience you had in being delivered or protected from evil attacks.

Meditate:
Pray today for protection and deliverance from evil forces.

3 foundations
&
3 functions

of a home
of prayer

DAY 29

Developing a spiritual self-image

You've probably never heard of the curse of thorns. I hadn't either until I heard the story of little Luke, a ten-year-old in India. Luke (not his real name) came to know Christ through a Children's Bible Club several years ago, and within a week of becoming a disciple he was at his grandmother's house telling her that he was going to break her curse of thorns. Twenty years earlier a witch doctor had cursed Grandma with this strange curse. On every "devil day," which was Thursday and Saturday, and on every new moon, Grandma could not walk because thornlike pain shot through every joint in her body. The fact that she was a cripple was an ongoing testimony to the power of the local witch doctor.

Everyone in the village knew why she could not walk on those two days each week, and they feared and dreaded the mysterious, dark, evil power that ruled the village through the priest.

Luke knew instinctively upon finding Christ that he had found a "greater power," and he hurried to his grandma's house. He told Grandma about giving his life to Christ and shared with her the fact that Christ could heal her. She only laughed and replied, "We have spent so much money in offerings to the priests to break this curse over the last twenty years. We have given so many chickens. But we have never found a power great enough to break the curse. I don't believe your new God can do it!"

But Luke persisted. He began to pray to his new God, Jesus. He had seen the power of Christ displayed in his little Children's Bible Club. He had seen other people healed. He knew that because he was a follower of Jesus, that power would flow through him.

As little Luke prayed for his grandmother, fire flowed through every joint in her body. It was a "devil day" and she was paralyzed, but gradually, as the prayers continued, she was able to move. The evil spell was being broken. Gingerly she stood up, and then with new confidence she stooped down to get through the little door of her hut and she began to walk and then dance down the dusty street.

The villagers flocked out of their homes and watched in awe for they had not seen her walk on a "devil day" for twenty years. "What has happened?" they shouted as she danced and jumped for joy. "How has the curse been broken?"

"My grandson prayed for me," she replied, "and his God heard his prayers. I can walk for the first time in twenty years."

"Who is this God?" they asked.

"I don't know!" Grandma shouted back. "You must ask him!" And so Luke had an opportunity to share all he had learned about Jesus in his ten-day Children's Bible Club program. He told about Christ's love and sacrifice for sins on the cross. He told about His resurrection from the dead. He is the God who rules all things today, even the evil powers that had placed the curse of thorns on his grandma. Most of villagers that day expressed a desire to find out more about this God, Jesus.

Luke knew instinctively, because he lived in India under the "rule" of the witch doctor, that when a person follows Christ he becomes a "royal priest." No, Luke had not heard this term found in 1 Peter 2:9. But that did not matter. He knew that through prayer he possessed a power to rule the evil spirits that had caused so much trouble for his grandma over the years.

Luke had a biblical (or spiritual) self-image that most of us lack. He saw himself as a spiritual ruler with immense, immeasurable spiritual power over evil. Most of us don't think of ourselves that way. We tend to think of ourselves as "only sinners saved by grace" and nothing more. We forget that we are "new creations in Christ Jesus" (see 2 Cor. 5:17); we are not being remodeled but re-created!

The Scriptures tell us that we were created *and redeemed* to be the rulers of the earth. Life now is a training period for that time when God will re-create the heavens and the earth, and we shall begin our rule, with Him, for eternity. We must regain the self-image that little Luke had; a self-image of courage and fearlessness. David had such a self-image as he faced Goliath, for he knew Who was on his side. David knew where his strength and authority over evil came from, and this authentic spiritual self-image motivated him to do something that appeared on a human level to be utterly irrational.

Homes **O**f **P**rayer **E**very day are families living in H.O.P.E.; that is, biblical hope. Biblical hope is a solid, exciting, certain anticipation of God's surprises. Our homes are the classrooms where Christ is training us to reign with Him for all eternity. In the next three meditations we will see the foundations of a **H**ome **O**f **P**rayer **E**very day as we explore three dimensions of a spiritual self-image. In the remaining three meditations this week we will see the three functions of a **H**ome **O**f **P**rayer **E**very day.

In this book, we have seen many aspects of what prayer is. Now we see another important facet of prayer—it is the instrument by which we rule the world. God gives prayer to us as the "scepter" of a king. As we point our prayers toward specific homes we begin to understand that we "rule" events with an unfathomable spiritual power: a divine power. When we pray, we become ruling priests. A priest is a person who offers prayers on behalf of his people, and in so doing rules. In this life we are being trained to reign for all eternity. The means by which we reign is prayer. Prayer is the link between a super-natural, all-powerful God and the material world. It is through the channel of prayer that God rules through us.

This week we will see our position as ruling priests. We have been given dominion over all the earth. We will see who we *really are* and be called back to our position of spiritual authority and inex-plicable, spiritual power. As you build your home into a **H**ome **O**f **P**rayer **E**very day, you are training the family to become ruling priests.

Reflect/Discuss:
What does it mean to be a "royal priest" (ruling by

prayer) in a secular world? What inexplicable incidents have occurred through your prayers, which show a divine, mysterious power at work? Why do Western Christian families often fail in using authoritative prayer as the primary tool in combating evil?

Meditate:

I am a spiritual ruler. The instrument (scepter) of my rule is prayer. I am being trained to reign with Christ for eternity.

DAY 30
Foundation #1: Knowing what we were

I believe that one of the greatest hindrances to prayer is our failure to realize our high position in God's creation. We seldom appreciate the fact that God made us humans to be superior beings. Paul alludes to our significance in God's hierarchy when he says that we will even judge angels (see 1 Cor. 6:1, 3). The story is told of C. S. Lewis being awakened one night by a noise in his living room. He went down the stairs and saw an apparition of the Devil sitting in the big chair. C. S. Lewis said, "Oh, it's only you!" and turned around and went to bed.

The Devil's goal is to fill us with fear and to crush us. He does not want us to know the truth that when God originally created us, He created us as:

His next of kin…
His likeness…
His appointed rulers…
His friends.

God's Next of Kin

Have you ever thought of yourself as God's "next of kin?" Thinking of yourself that way does not mean you are God. It does mean that you are God's child. Children, while related to parents, are distinct. They are not the parents. They are their own persons. So too, as God's next of kin we are related to God, but we are not God.

What does this image mean in our approach to daily life? We are God's next of kin! We are His children. If you were the "next of kin" to the ruler of your nation, would that not have a positive effect on your outlook? The Devil wants to crush our self-image. He lies to us, telling us that we are nothing but dust—that we're evil, sinful failures. He certainly does not want us to consider our position in creation.

To be God's next of kin means a host of things,

not the least of which is the capacity to love and relate to Him. We are spirits as He is a Spirit. We are persons as He is a Person. We can walk together, talk together, and share together. We can be wrapped in His love because God calls Himself our Father and our elder Brother.

Perhaps the most glorious of all pictures in Scripture illustrating the fact that we are God's next of kin is found in a little known verse, Zephaniah 3:17: "He will take great delight in you, he will quiet you with his love, he will rejoice over you with singing." Have you ever thought of yourself as being that close to God that He rejoices over you with singing as a mother coos over her child?

Establishing a **H**ome **O**f **P**rayer **E**very day begins with climbing in God's lap (see Day 2) and letting His arms of love enfold you!

God's Likeness

When God created Adam and Eve, He not only created them as His next of kin, but He created them to be like Him; He created us in His likeness (see Genesis 1:26). Just what does this mean? It means that we look like God in some ways. We look like God through our loving each other and caring for each other. We look like God in our capacity to forgive. We look like God in our capacity to suffer for one another. Think of yourself as someone who looks like God; who sees as God sees; who is an "advisor" to God through prayer, pointing out needs to Him!

God's Appointed Rulers

When we were first created God gave us a position of "ruling over" every aspect of creation. All creatures and all plant life were placed under us so that we could exhibit God's likeness in caring for them and developing them. As you pray, you are learning how to rule with Christ in the spiritual realm. A good ruler protects his people, provides resources for his people, and brings peace to his people. These are the three functions of a "ruling priest." We will see that in the last three meditations this week.

God's Friends

Finally, Adam and Eve had the capability of being God's friends. In some mysterious way God came to them "in the cool of the evening" and talked with them on a regular basis. Prayer is the primary channel through which we express friendship with God just as communication through speech is the main linkage of all friends. We become friends when we talk with each other and through communication are motivated then to care for each other in other ways.

Reflect/Discuss:

Why do we seldom reflect on what God has made us to be?

Meditate:

I am God's relative; His likeness; His appointed ruler; His companion and friend!

Foundation #2: Knowing what we are in Christ

When Adam and Eve sinned and refused relationship with God, He did not reject them; He redeemed them in Christ. What's especially remarkable is that in Christ He took us to an even higher level than the level of creation. If we wish to learn to pray, we must be aware of who and what we are. Until we understand that we are more than mere sinners saved by grace, we will never enter into the authority and power of our unique relationship with the King of kings. Prayer will remain little more than begging and not be the "scepter" of power by which we rule the universe.

New Creation

Perhaps one of the greatest tools of Satan has

been the lie that we are "merely sinners saved by grace." Paul tells us, "Therefore, if anyone is in Christ, he is a new creation; the old has gone, the new has come!" (2 Cor. 5:17). To be born again by God's Spirit means that His Spirit forms a "new creation" within us. God's Spirit cannot create sin. Thus, within us lies a new, sinless creation, growing and emerging; that condition is totally of God. We are not being remodeled. We are not being "helped" to live a new life. God has created new life within us. It is His work. We are responsible for setting the conditions for the development and growth of this new life and for the putting off of the old. "Do not conform any longer to the pattern of this world, but be transformed by the renewing of your mind" (Rom. 12:2). It is in this new life that we are learning to reign and rule over the universe. As we pray, we must come to Christ not merely as forgiven sinners, but also remembering what He has redeemed us to be.

The Bride of Christ

Christ describes a remarkable height to which

humans are redeemed when they are called the "Bride of Christ" (see Rev. 21:1–2). In all cultures a woman is most beautifully dressed at her wedding. Our relationship to Christ is so intimate and so beautiful that Paul uses the tender love relationship of husband and wife to describe it. "Husbands, love your wives, just as Christ loved the church and gave himself up for her" (Eph. 5:25).

Christ has chosen to reveal His beauty to the world through His "bride." This is why a praying family is especially important. Each family unit is to show the kind of spiritual family Christ is creating. In the family's tender acts of love and kindness and in her strength in prohibiting the spread of evil, that family reveals the beauty of the Savior. As we pray and offer ourselves as the conduits through which the answers flow, we reveal the beauty of Christ.

The Brothers and Sisters of Christ

If your brother were ruler of a great nation, your position in life would be dramatically changed. Our Brother may not be ruler of your nation, but He is

the King of kings and Lord of lords! He is a
loving Brother, and we are His family, His royalty!

Newly created, bride, and brothers…

We are redeemed to be more than God's likeness
and next of kin; more than rulers and companions.
Through our salvation in Christ and His atoning work
He has made us to be His new creations, His bride,
and His brothers and sisters. These pictures show
how God has generously and graciously used salvation to defeat Satan and lift us to an even higher
level in the order of the universe. One cannot
over-emphasize our closeness to God after Christ's
redemption. We are new creations—His bride,
His family.

Reflect/Discuss:
*How do this and the previous meditations increase
your motivation to pray?*

Meditate:
*Think about your relationship to Christ as His newly
created bride, and brother or sister.*

Foundation #3: Knowing what we shall be

Have you ever wondered why God doesn't tell us more about heaven? John says, "Dear friends, now we are children of God, and what we will be has not yet been made known. But we know that when he appears, we shall be like him, for we shall see him as he is" (1 John 3:2).

One of the most positive, powerful memories of my childhood centers on Christmas presents. We had little growing up, and perhaps that's why Christmas presents were so important. We had few toys and, unlike many families today, did not get things on a regular basis. My parents were very good at keeping secrets, and a week before Christmas the presents would be placed under the tree. The four children would try to guess what was in them, examining them, weighing them, wondering about their shapes and sizes. Anticipation would build daily as our parents refused to tell us what they had purchased. That hope and anticipation was such a major part of growing up. I don't remember many of the presents, but I do remember with great clarity the excitement of anticipating the moment when we could open them.

I think God deals with us in the same way when it comes to heaven. He has a "Christmas present" called heaven waiting for each of us. He has shown us, as we have seen in the last two meditations, both what He has created us to be and also what He has redeemed us to be. But what we shall be… well, He is keeping that under wraps, wanting us, His little children, to trust Him and live in excited anticipation of His goodness as we wonder what it will be like. God wants our "certainty" about the future to rest in Him, not in what He is doing.

However, as John reports in 1 John 3:2, we do know something about heaven; namely, that we will be like Christ when He appears. Wow! We will be like our Savior? That is enough to make any Christian excited. Think of His resurrection appearances and power. Think of His ascension and position in glory. Think of His appearance as the Man clothed in white as John reported Him in Revelation 1:14–16.

Heaven's Rewards

In the parable of the talents (see Luke 19:10–27) Christ tells us clearly that there will be different levels or different rewards for believers, depending on their success during this earthly period of training. Some will be placed over ten cities, some over five, and some will be saved as if by fire. There is a believer's judgment in which heavenly rewards are determined. Are we striving for those rewards as Paul did?

Yes, we are in training now to rule for eternity. Our homes are our classrooms. We are being trained to reign using the scepter of prayer. And we are to pour all our energies into learning how to rule through prayer.

Paul says that he counts everything as rubbish in order to gain this reward (see Phil. 3:8). He presses on, he strains to reach the goal of the prize. He wants to know or experience not only the power of Christ's resurrection, but also the fellowship of His sufferings (see Phil. 3:10).

I cannot help but think of the sports craze that afflicts so many Christian families. Even one of the leading sports magazines carried an article by a non-Christian, lamenting the fact that sports have become so all consuming that we even give up our Sundays for them. Our children train and train and train to win the soccer or Little League ball games.

But what about spiritual training in our homes? Are we teaching our children who they really are? Are we providing the motivation to rule? Are we training them to use prayer as the scepter of their ruling? We are not created and redeemed to be slaves; we're dominion keepers, ruling the world through our prayer-union with Jesus Christ.

Paul tells Timothy in 2 Timothy 2:12 that if we endure we will also reign with Christ. Christ tells the church in Thyatira, "To him who overcomes and does my will to the end, I will give authority over the nations…" (Rev. 2:26). And Christ's concluding word to the Laodiceans is, "To him who overcomes, I will give the right to sit with me on my throne, just as I overcame and sat down with my Father on his throne" (Rev. 3:21).

Summary:

These are the three foundations on which we build a **H**ome **O**f **P**rayer **E**very day. They are the three foundations of knowing what we were created to be, what we have been redeemed to be, and now, what we are being trained to be. We are being trained to reign with Christ for all eternity. The primary instrument of our reign is the instrument of prayer. The more we learn to use it, the more reward will be ours in glory!

Reflect/Discuss:

Compare the amount of time and energy that an average Christian family devotes to sports with the amount of time and energy devoted to learning to reign through prayer.

Meditate:

Reflect on who God made you to be; who God redeemed you to be; and what you shall become in the next life.

Function #1:
Prohibiting evil

We have seen the three foundations of a **H**ome **O**f **P**rayer **E**very day in reviewing who God created us to be, who He redeemed us to be, and what we are being trained to become. These three great areas of truth form the foundation, the motivation, the basis for making our homes H.O.P.E.

We are ready next to look at the three functions of a **H**ome **O**f **P**rayer **E**very day. Jesus teaches these three functions in Matthew 18:18–20. "I tell you this: Whatever you prohibit on earth is prohibited in heaven, and whatever you allow on earth is allowed in heaven. I also tell you this: If two of you agree down here on earth concerning anything you ask, my Father in heaven will do it for you. For where two or three gather together because they are mine, I am there among them" (NLT).

Christ touches on three subjects in this passage: prohibiting destructive evil, divine provision of needs, and His presence among believers. These three activities, prohibiting evil through prayer, prviding for needs supernaturally through prayer, and bringing the presence of Christ through prayer are the three basic functions of a **H**ome **O**f **P**rayer **E**very day.

The first function is prohibiting evil through prayer. And when Jesus taught that "whatever you allow on earth is allowed in heaven," that included even demonic activity. This function is vividly illustrated in the following story. Daniel is a church planter working in Southern India among moonshiners (illicit liquor makers) and prostitutes. He began his work in this area in 1996 and continued until 2000. The area was utterly, morally degraded. Alcoholism abounded. Family abuse was common. And Daniel's approach was, "Accept Christ or go to hell!" He shouted it, screamed it, and proclaimed it, but to no avail. Nothing happened.

In 2000 Daniel was accepted into one of Mission

India's Institute of Community Transformation classes (church planting) and learned how to "prohibit" Satan's activity in the area where he was working. He learned that he had to prohibit Satan and his demons, first, before starting to witness.

This work required some research. He had to visit the people in the village and establish a loving, caring relationship with them. He had to learn their stories—their heartaches and disappointments. He had to come to know what they felt their needs were and why they lived in such horrible conditions. His vision, he was told, had to match the needs of the people he was trying to reach.

So he stopped preaching and started to listen. That's probably the first and most important lesson about witnessing. Don't talk! Listen! He learned who his people were and what they needed. In the process Daniel also learned who their gods and goddesses were. In India that is a bit easier to do than in the West since they take the form of visible idols. He identified two male idols and two female idols.

Once he had identified them, Daniel walked

around the area in which he was ministering, prohibiting or binding these gods and goddesses from continuing their destructive work. He realized, through his training, what he really was in Christ. He was not "merely a sinner saved by grace" but a royal priest operating from his spiritual position of being "in" the King of kings. From this position of rule he had the authority and power to prohibit the demonic spirits from further activity in the village. As he prohibited them here on earth, in this specific little area in southern India, these demonic spirits were also prohibited in the heavenly realms.

Daniel knew when these entities were prohibited from further control of the area. He was amazed that within a very short time, those who had paid no attention to him and who had disregarded his harsh and loveless message, suddenly changed. It seemed as if the prison doors had been opened and slowly the prisoners were walking out of spiritual darkness.

One of the first signs that the prohibition was working came through a woman fortune-teller—a priestess. This woman had built a small brick temple with a thatched roof. She lived most of the day in a confused, trance-like, drunken state, muttering to herself and making little sense. Her sister's husband became very ill and she could not heal him. Daniel was brought in and told her that he was a priest as she was and the God he served could heal her brother-in-law.

Daniel then prayed and God answered. Daniel laid hands on her and commanded the demons to leave. Immediately her confusion and trance-like state was changed. Her eyes became clear. A smile graced her face and an unknown, miraculous joy and peace flooded her heart. She accepted Christ. Her husband became a disciple too, as did her daughter. And she stood in front of the church of over one hundred ex-prostitutes and moonshiners the day I preached there. I saw her radiating the marvelous joy of Christ that comes when the Devil is prohibited from working.

There are homes in the West that are being torn down with the help of demonic activity. Quarreling, fighting, and selfishness work to cause division and divorce, and sometimes evil spiritual forces will augment and further the destructive work of sin in individuals. Perhaps the greatest tragedy is the fact that the Christians of the West seem as caught up in the wreckage of homes as non-Christians.

In creating a **H**ome **O**f **P**rayer **E**very day one of the first functions is to join together in prayer, claiming victory over evil and pleading with Christ for the supernatural power of the Holy Spirit. Our homes could be radically transformed if we would become more serious and disciplined in using our powerful scepter of prayer to prohibit evil (be it of spiritual forces, of the world's system, or of our own flesh) in our homes each day. Are you having difficulty in your family? The answer is to make your home a **H**ome **O**f **P**rayer **E**very day! Try it for thirty days! God will be faithful.

Reflect/Discuss:
While the prohibition of demonic activity is common in India and other countries, it is relatively unknown in

the West. Have you encountered it or experienced it? What is your attitude toward it? What are the dangers of working in this area?

Meditate:
In what areas of your life is there a need to "prohibit" demonic activity?

Function #2: Providing resources

I love motor homes. I've only had two, very old ones. But I'm hooked on reading want ads and stopping at RV lots. I'm always looking, always dreaming. And one day in all my looking I came across a very old, Dodge motor home in very bad shape. If you know anything about motor homes you will remember that those early Dodges had a rounded shape. This thing must have been thirty years old. The dealer wanted an outrageous price for it. It was in terrible condition, and I wondered how anyone in good conscience could ask so much for such a pile of junk.

A year later I used the illustration of that motor home in a speech. After the talk a young mother came up and excitedly told me that she and her husband had purchased that very motor home. I was a little taken aback by that information, and asked her what she had done with it. She said they spent the entire winter getting it back in shape and at spring break they, with their six kids, had driven it from Michigan to Florida. I asked her how she made out.

"Fantastic" was her reply. "The old thing broke down twelve times!" "And you said that was fantastic?" I asked. "Yes. It was a fabulous spiritual experience for all of us. The first time it broke down, we pulled over and got the kids in a circle, kneeling together on the floor and praying that God would send someone to help us. God did! It was incredible. It happened a second time, and God delivered us. It was so exciting that after the fourth time the kids started to pray that the thing would break down again so we could see how God would help us. It was an experience in God's divine provision that our six children will never forget!"

That crazy story is true and carries a profound point. How many of us, in our family life, ever develop this kind of child-like trust in the Lord? How many of us have circumstances in which we can see His immediate, strange, and inexplicable provision?

One of the quickest and most discernable ways to experience God's provision is to pray for miraculous amounts of money for missions. In 1967, in my second pastorate, I was leading a youth group whose boredom was only exceeded by my own. I decided that something striking had to be done to rescue this impossible situation. So I asked how many of them believed in miracles. They all said without much excitement that they believed in miracles.

I then asked them how many had seen a miracle. None of them felt they had.

I asked a third question. "How many would like to see a miracle?" That finally got their interest, and they asked how it would be possible. "Does God just have a shelf full of miracles?"

I said He did and that the reason we failed to see them was that we did not ask for one of them. I said, "Why don't you ask God for $10,000 to build a church in Taiwan?" (My total salary then was only

$6,000!) They laughed at the totally ridiculous idea, but then decided to pray and after prayer to vote. The vote was unanimous: they would ask God to use them to raise $10,000, an amount about equal to $100,000 today.

They asked each family in the church to save loose change in a little bank and join them in asking God to miraculously provide the money. They asked only for pennies, nickels, dimes, and quarters. And they promised to pick up the change monthly for the next twelve months. They quit after just ten months, having collected not $10,000 but $12,500, and every other fund in the church was over budget!

Since that time we've encouraged families (often through youth groups and Sunday Schools) to save loose change in "rice bags," following the example of poor Christians in India who save a handful of rice each day. On Sunday they take the rice to church as their offering. We encourage them to do this for eight or sixteen weeks. Churches have collected as much as $40,000 to send 40,000 kids in India to two-week Children's Bible Clubs.[2]

What are you doing in your home to experience God's miraculous provision? What are your specific needs? Remember who you are—you are God's likeness, His image bearer, and the receiver of His promises. When you gather in unity to ask God to provide so that you can do His work, you have His promise in Matthew 18:19 that He will hear and He will answer. It is in the area of God's supernatural provision that provides some of the greatest excitement and powerful reasons for hope.

Reflect/Discuss:
What are some of your experiences as a family in God's miraculous provision? What are some challenges you face in having God provide for you now? What are you doing in missions in asking God for supernatural provision to make disciples?

Meditation:
"Again, I tell you that if two of you on earth agree about anything you ask for, it will be done for you by my Father in heaven" (Matt. 18:19).

Function #3: Bringing the presence of Christ

My wife held our youngest grandchild on her lap. He was three years old. Since he lived some eight hundred miles from us, we got to see him only two or three times a year. He was waiting, all smiles, as we came down the escalator in the airport. He made a mad dash for us the moment we stepped off. He was so excited all the way home that he never stopped talking.

Later that night, just before bedtime, as Grandma held him in her lap, he looked up at her and said, "You know why we's so happy, Gram?"

And Grandma replied, "No, why?"

With a grin from ear to ear he said, "Cause you's here!"

The gift of the presence of a loved one is without doubt the single most precious possession. Anyone who has lost a close relative can testify to that. The loneliness resulting from a spouse's death is beyond description. The presence of a loved one is the highest treasure of life. Why is it that even after bitter divorce people still want to get married again? We desperately need companionship, for we are created in God's image!

Thus, when the angel told Joseph, "and they will call him Immanuel—which means, 'God with us,'" he was talking about the greatest gift God could give to us; namely, the gift of His own presence.

Have you experienced the "presence" of God through worship, or through a time of special trial, or in a time of special joy? I remember the days in the early seventies when my wife and I were first introduced to "home worship" by a group of recent converts. They were meeting each week for praise, and since they were new to the Christian faith they desired a second meeting for Bible study each week. We led the Bible study in our home and in return went to their worship time in their home. In their worship meeting they sang with feeling the likes of which we had never experienced before, and we felt the presence of Christ in a marvelous new way. That experience of the presence of Christ lingers in us to this day as an experience of what heaven will be like.

The function of a **H**ome **O**f **P**rayer **E**very day is not merely to prohibit evil within the family, and to create excitement and confidence about the ways in which God provides for us, but also it is to bring us all, as a family, into the presence of Christ. When we are washed with the presence of the Savior, our problems and quarrels, our anxieties and irritations all fall away. Grudges are forgiven. Unity comes.

A Catholic priest said that his native village in Italy had very few divorces due to the "the wedding crosses." As part of each wedding ceremony, the newly married couple was given a cross to hang on the wall of their apartment: a wedding cross. It had a very special function. Whenever they got in a fight, one of them was to run to the cross, take it down, hold it, and the fighting was to stop immediately. They promised in the wedding ceremony that they would get on their knees and pray for the presence of Christ to dispel fighting. Most of the couples were faithful, and fights and quarrels ended in love and harmony because Christ came and washed them with the love of His presence.

How many of the promises of God center on His covenant to be with us, to bless us with His presence? "For where two or three come together in my name, there am I with them" (Matt. 18:20). This is a core promise; all other promises flow from it. Nothing is more important than that the God who IS love dwells within us in His loving presence.

We were walking in the woods one day with another of our grandchildren. The little fellow would not hold our hands, but insisted on wandering off, far ahead or to the side or lagging behind. He was fascinated with all the bugs and spiders. He was shocked into tears, however, when a large snake suddenly slithered across his path, and he came running back to us, grabbing for our hands.

He needed to hold our hands at that moment. He needed the assurance of our presence.

God promises the same to us. "This is what God the LORD says, he who created the heavens and stretched them out, who spread out the earth and all that comes out of it, who gives breath to its people, and life to those who walk on it: 'I, the LORD, have called you in righteousness; *I will take hold of your hand*'" (Isa. 42:5–6). Think back to the second meditation—riding on the tractor with the Lord. Remember that prayer is something more than words, it is a relationship with God. It is the relationship pictured in God, the Father of mankind, knowing our name, calling us, and saying, "I will hold your hand."

"Now the dwelling of God is with me, and he will live with them. They will be his people, and God himself will be with them and be their God. He will wipe every tear from their eyes. There will be no more death or mourning or crying or pain" (Rev. 21:3–4).

"And they will call him Immanuel—which means, 'God with us'" (Matt. 1:23).

Make your home a **H**ome **O**f **P**rayer **E**very day. As you pray together ask God to prohibit the evil forces of Satan, the world, and your own flesh from working in your relationships—bind the power of evil in prayer. Learn how to rule over sin through the instrument of prayer. Praying together, experience the miraculous provision of Christ. And most of all, move to the highest experience of a human, that of the presence of Christ in your family in moments of worship and praise.

Reflect/Discuss:
Describe the most memorable experience you have had with the presence of God.

Meditate:
Picture yourself as going through the day holding the hand of God!

building a
home of prayer
every day

DAY 36
The vision
of H.O.P.E.

I've always been fascinated with the word "hope." Perhaps this fascination comes because I dreaded going to heaven as a little boy. I couldn't decide what was worse—eternity in hell fire or eternity resting and playing harps. Hell sounded terrible, but heaven wasn't much better. I hated naps and playing the piano, and doing that for eternity was no more appealing than the alternative!

It wasn't until I understood that all my "hopes" would not be fulfilled in heaven that I got over my dread of it. I came to understand that I would still be able to anticipate things in heaven, and that sounded downright exciting. I would be able to "grow" in heaven, expand in exciting ways.

Dad was the person who pointed it out to me

when, as a chemist, he said that he would have an eternity of experiments in heaven, each more exciting than the last and each pointing out ever-increasing revelations of the greatness of God. He also taught me that the excitement would never wane or grow cold as it does on earth. Heaven would be filled with *living hope*, which means we will never be disappointed. He had good Biblical grounds for his belief in eternal hope: 1 Corinthians 13:13! "And now these three remain: faith, hope and love." Hope remains, along with faith and love, through eternity!

Hope means anticipation. It really is the essence of life. It also means growth. Children live in "hope" with excited, positive expectations of growing up. They hope (look forward) to their next birthday, counting the years in terms of months or weeks or even days. What person doesn't remember with fondness the "hope" or anticipation of Christmas?

On the other hand, when we no longer have positive expectations about the future, we have ceased to experience life. Arguably, depression is a kind of absence of hope.

The Vision of H.O.P.E.

I think a case could be made for saying that "hope" is a synonym for prayer! As a matter of fact, hope is to prayer what a wick is to a firecracker. You cannot light a firecracker without a wick any more than you can pray without hope. Hope launches prayer. Prayer without excited expectations of what God will do is prayer prayed without faith. James comments on hopeless prayer as follows: "But when he asks, he must believe and not doubt, because he who doubts is like a wave of the sea, blown and tossed by the wind. That man should not think he will receive anything from the Lord; he is a double-minded man, unstable in all he does" (James 1:6–8).

Thus my acronym H.O.P.E. has a double implication. Not only does it refer to the structure or means by which we pray effectively, but the word also explains the excitement of prayer. Praying in faith is praying in hope. Faith means that we expect God to answer, anticipate God's answers, and look forward to God's answers. He will answer our prayers in ways we cannot ask or imagine (see Eph. 3:20). The most precious gift for our children is the gift of living hope. And the vision of a **H**ome **O**f **P**rayer **E**very day is a vision of having a family characterized by hope.

The Need of a Vision of H.O.P.E.

Do you have a vision of bringing "hope" to your family? Making your home a **H**ome **O**f **P**rayer **E**very day will result in the gift of a positive, excited, hope-filled attitude toward life. Nothing will drive out anxiety, depression, fighting, and division as a regular time of prayer and praise together. Nothing will correct our view of life as does being washed in the presence of Christ when two or three gather in worship. Probably the single most important vision you could have right now is the vision of making your home a **H**ome **O**f **P**rayer **E**very day.

Bhopal, a city in India, was the site of the Union Carbide disaster, which killed thousands in one night years ago. It has been known throughout India as the City of Death. When the Christians in the city heard about the concept of H.O.P.E. (**H**ome **O**f **P**rayer **E**very day) they not only received a vision of putting homes of prayer everywhere in Bhopal, but they decided to "rename" their city: Bhopal, City of H.O.P.E.

The Need of God's Vision of H.O.P.E.

There are four marks which characterize a home of prayer: prayer (praise), share, care, and dare. In the remaining four meditations we will review each one with the prayer that these four things may characterize your home.

Reflect/Discuss:

Talk about making your home a home of prayer with family members. Draw up a vision statement for the family of what you expect to happen in your home and in the homes you will be praying for.

Meditate:

Will you and your family choose to make your home a home of prayer?

Step #1: Prayer as praise

The first step in making your home a **H**ome **O**f **P**rayer **E**very day is to lead all family members into true praise, the beginning of every vital prayer. One of the best instructions on praise is given in Psalm 145. In the opening verses, David, the author of the Psalm, tells us that he has made up his mind to praise God. *I will praise God*, he says. He repeats his decision three times. *I will praise, I will praise, I will praise*. Praise of God is not something that happens to us. Rather, it is something that we make happen by a rational decision. How many decisions do you make each day in your home? Shouldn't praising God be one of those decisions?

But how do we go about praising God in our family? What do we do? Here are five simple steps you can take to get your family started in meaningful praise. Of course, before taking these five steps, make the decision that you are going to have a time of praise.

Make the decision that you, as a family, will praise God together. So, get everyone together and read the following steps.

#1: Exalt God!

That's a fancy way of saying, "Let's think about God for the next few moments. Nothing else. Let's focus our minds on His character and on His greatness. In our family we talk about sports, about politics, about the church, about music…let's talk about God now." Then read through Psalm 145 and stop at every verse for comments. Ask for opinions on how to do what the verse suggests. Sing a few praise songs together. Have we experienced the things the psalmist is praising God for? How?

#2: Enjoy God!

People who have experienced true praise in a small group, such as a family setting, know that there is no more enjoyable experience in all of human life! Praising God is the most moving thing that can happen to us.

One of the highlights of my spiritual life was a prayer conference with seventy other pastors. When I got there, I was shocked to learn that we would be praying for three days; not speaking about prayer and watching videos. I was desperate to get out. But all of us found that the experience not only was among the most enjoyable ones of our spiritual life, but we also did not want it to end three days later. We sat in a circle, spontaneously praying, singing, reading Scripture, and yes, laughing together. We had times of crying as we confessed sins also, but that would never have happened had we not prayed.

Pastor and author John Piper explains his "conversion" in terms of learning to enjoy God. He said that his family would discuss and enjoy everything— sports, church, work, play. But when he finally learned to enjoy God, he came into an experience more pleasurable than anything he had ever imagined (*Desiring God*. Multnomah, 1986).

Bathe this first meeting in prayer together as parents. Reflect on personal reasons why you want to praise God. Perhaps there is something that you have never before shared with the family.

#3: Be Excited About God!

I remember so well a Good Friday service in a large Assembly of God church in our town. It was led by a pastor of a noncharismatic church; a union service of all evangelicals. He had an excellent message in which he acted out his last point. He showed that Jesus died, rose again, and ascended into heaven. And when He ascended… then the pastor stopped and, without a word, got a folding chair, opened it, and sat down. The crowd went wild as they saw their Savior, in that action, entering heaven and "sitting down" in a place of supreme victory and glory! Talk about excitement—they shouted and whistled and stamped their feet. It was as wild if not wilder than any ball game I've attended.

No, you probably don't want that much excitement in your home, but you do want your family to be excited about what God is doing. What do you think the families who go to Daniel's church (see Day 33) feel when they see how God has been answering their prayers? I think they are so excited that they naturally are telling others.

Ask God to bring a sense of excitement to all of you in this meeting. Don't be afraid to be quiet. Be spontaneous. When you pray and someone mentions a reason for praise, follow up on that reason. Add to it with a short prayer.

#4: Have Great Expectations of What God Will Do.

Remember the story of the old motor home breaking down twelve times on the way to Florida? Remember how the kids got so excited about how God answered their prayers each time, that they started to pray for the old crate to break down?

It is so easy to get your children to have great expectations about what God is going to do. Set a goal for the number of children you could send to a Children's Bible Club in India at just one dollar apiece. Then start your children saving their loose change. You do it with them. Perhaps you can pray for other income. And then rejoice together in what God does for you.

I remember well the schoolteacher in my church who saved $1,000 for a new piece of furniture, but got so excited at a missions conference that he gave the entire amount in the offering. That very night, visiting a friend who was a furniture maker, he saw the "break-front" he wanted in his home. The furniture maker said that he made it out of scraps of wood and wanted to give it away to someone who appreciated it! He gave it to the schoolteacher.

God moves in such mysterious ways, beyond all expectations. Are you filling your children with great expectations of how God is moving?

#5: I will Extol God.

Extol is an old English word for sharing God. Do you dream of having your family so full of praise to God, enjoying God so much and being so excited and filled with great expectations, that they share God naturally, without thinking or being trained for it? That's what we are seeing happen in India. These homes are homes of praise, thanking God for miracles of transformation. And the members of the families are so filled with excitement and awe that they are sharing this God with other families, and those families are making homes of prayer every day. So the Gospel sweeps over the nation!

Remember that there are three forms of prayer: petition, praise, and a position of child-like trust and confidence. Prayer is first of all a position or relationship with Christ, which can be expressed in words and songs of praise and petition.

Reflect/Discuss:
Try doing the five steps of praise as a family.

Meditate:
We were made to know God and enjoy Him forever! In what ways do you enjoy God?

Step #2: C.A.R.E.

Free to Choose by Milton and Rose Freidman, had remained on my bookshelf, unread, for twenty years. I finally got around to reading it the other day and was shocked that while it is a book on economics, it has a profound theological significance. In it the authors develop Adam Smith's theory of equal exchange of value.

It starts with the simple explanation that I have a pencil and you have fifty cents. We exchange values equally when you give me fifty cents and I give you the pencil. It is this little equation which makes the "world go round." The authors show how lines of communication develop without pre-planning around the exchange of value for a wooden pencil, reaching to the forests of the Northwest for the wood, and the rubber plantations of Indonesia for the eraser, and the graphite mines of Sri Lanka for the lead. Change the price of the pencil, and all areas are immediately affected. A natural communication system is set up based on profits. They even push further, showing how the lumber industry provides wood for the pencils, reaches out to supporting industries for machinery, markets, advertisements, and ships. Everything starts the ball rolling with the freedom given to exchange equal value.

As I meditated on that idea, I thought about the principle theologically. Is this theory more than merely a simple explanation of economics? Is there an underlying principle describing all human relationships here? Could we substitute the word C.A.R.E. (Caring And Receiving care Equally) for the concept of the exchange of value? Doesn't "caring and receiving care equally" describe all human relationships? And isn't friendship built on the equal exchange of care? Are not families, groups of friends, and small groups generally built around the principle that in these "communities" we are both cared for and dignified in giving equal (reciprocal, not identical) care to others?

Think about how "caring and receiving care equally" applied to Adam and Eve. It gives a new insight into the nature of sin. God gave the entire world to Adam and Eve as His expression of care for them. All the days of creation led up to the climax, the creation of man in God's own image and likeness. At the climax God gave all creation to Adam and Eve, charging them to care for it and have dominion over it.

In return God asked Adam and Eve to care for Him. They were to show this care by obeying Him. This obedience consisted of freely denying themselves the forbidden fruit. Thus a two-way, caring relationship would be set up. God gave Himself totally in caring for them, and they were to care for God in return by putting their desires aside and loving Him through their obedience.

While Adam and Eve were willing to receive God's care, they refused to return their "care" to God. They showed this refusal in disobeying God's command. Not only did they demand all that God had already given them, but they also demanded that God give them the forbidden fruit as well. They refused to care for God, wanting only His care for them. No "equal exchange of care" occurred. Their love relationship with God was broken. Remember the meditation in Day 3 about holding hands with God? We are united with God in an eternal bond only when there is an equal exchange of care. The folding of one hand into another, as in prayer, is a symbol of equal care. God cares for us; we are to care for God through obedience and faith in return. When this equal exchange occurs we live forever. When we fail in caring for God as did Adam and Eve, we break our relationship and live in eternal isolation from Him.

All human relationships, as well as our relationship with God, are based on this concept of the equal exchange of care. A happy marriage is the union of a man and woman who care for each other "equally" throughout all of life. Marital problems occur when the "care dial" is lopsided and one partner feels that he or she does all the caring while the other lives in selfishness.

How much of life is spent lamenting the "imbalance" of care. Gossip spreads about selfishness of others. We are indignant about ways in which people can expect so much from us and give so little in return. All relationships focus on getting the balance of care set equally.

Care must be given *and received* equally. There is an important warning here, for Christians often emphasize only caring for others. They do not realize that care can degrade if it does not open up the opportunity for the care receiver *to return equal care*. When the return of care is not forthcoming we may breed "parasitism" as is bred by welfare.

When we make our home a **H**ome **O**f **P**rayer **E**very day, we not only bring hope but also C.A.R.E. (**C**aring **A**nd **R**eceiving care **E**qually). We will have an opportunity to openly discuss the need not only to care for others, but to receive "equal" care in return. We can discuss how we destroy people and relationships when we only care for them and ask nothing in return. Remember back to the meditation about walking in step with Christ (Day 9)? In that meditation we learned that we walk with two legs—one the leg of prayer and the other the leg of work.

A **H**ome **O**f **P**rayer **E**very day is not merely about prayer but also about working or caring. It is about the work of loving *and receiving love*. As we meet in prayer we should discuss the proper balance of equal caring that forms healthy relationships, beginning in our home. We should warn our children against destroying the dignity of others by merely giving care and not allowing or encouraging an equal return of care. We should, in our prayer times, be aware of the balance of equal care for each other. We must understand that the essence of sin, as demonstrated by Adam and Eve, is to merely take God's care without returning our care to him.

Reflect/Discuss:
What do you like about the C.A.R.E. principle?

Meditate:
"Think of ways to encourage one another to outbursts of love and good deeds" (Heb. 10:25 NLT).

Step #3:
Share

A praising, caring family will be a sharing family. Sharing is an art, a discipline. So often Christians are proclaiming, not sharing people. We shout out the Good News with insensitivity. Even in our own homes, we tend to thrust the Gospel down the throats of our loved ones. We need to understand that sharing doesn't start with stating our opinion. Sharing begins with listening.

Remember the story of Daniel, the church planter, who said the first thing he learned was that his vision didn't match the people he was trying to reach. He researched his village. He finally learned to keep his mouth shut and listen as people described their concerns to him. As Christians we need to learn to keep our mouths shut. And, at times we must learn to keep our mouths shut in our families.

Sharing means first of all learning about the other person. What hurts is that person experiencing? What joys?

Nowhere is there a more natural platform to learn how to share than in the family! One of our children has the occasional habit of going around the table after dinner asking the simple question, "What was good about your day?" Each person gets all the time needed to answer. It doesn't go smoothly all the time, but it is a learning experience that trains the family members to listen to each other. It trains them to understand that others' opinions count.

We also need to share God's Word with one another. A Home of Prayer is a place where we encourage each other to outbursts of love and joy (see Heb. 10:24 NLT), and these outbursts are the result of discovering God's promises and directions together in His Word.

The Four Steps

Several years ago my wife and I discovered a set of four simple questions that enable you to discover the meaning of any passage of the Bible and apply it to your life. These four questions can be used to help you share in family devotions.

1. "What did you like best in this study?" This is the question that removes all tension about being right or wrong. It is an opinion question, which puts people at ease and allows them freedom not only to express their thoughts but also to go deeper and express their life story. It shows that you care for them and are allowing them… rather, inviting them to return the care as an equal, by sharing their opinion.

Encourage multiple answers to the question. There may be several things people like. You might even write them down, reviewing them frequently. Encourage each person who answers by remarks such as, "What a terrific insight… that's really a neat observation," etc. This first question probably might take the majority of time in Bible study and sharing with each other.

A salesman whom I trained in this method got so excited about it that he used it in sales. He put his product on the counter and asked the customer what he liked about it. He said that he never had to say anything—the customer "sold himself." And, when a person discovers a truth, rather than having it pronounced to him, that truth becomes far more precious. Remember, seed needs to be planted in holes, and questions are the shovels that open a person's spirit to receive the Word of God.

2. "What don't you like or don't you understand?" This question gives the person the right to express difficulties or doubts. Share your struggles in prayer with each other. Be open. The only way you can deal with doubt is to bring it out in the open. Don't rush in with your opinions and answers! Dig with your questions. Remember that Christ (and the rabbis) taught with stories called parables. They made the people discover the meaning on their own!

3. "What did you learn about God?" All meetings should be "God" oriented and reflect on discoveries about God. This point may not require much time in your family, but it could also be an opportunity to return to praise. Make certain, by the way, that a spirit of praise and hopefulness fills all you do in this time of family devotions.

4. "What must we do?" This final question deals with practical steps, deeds, which must be accomplished during the period until your prayer team meets again. Not only should you lay out specific actions, but when you meet you must report on fulfilling these actions. Mission India's training programs consist of three parts: Learn it, do it, and report it. A family is an excellent setting not only to hammer out a practical application of what a passage means but also to report on putting it into practice.

5. Summarize: As the discussion draws to a close, ask the family to decide on an overall theme of the passage or story and perhaps to suggest a few sub points for that theme.

This method of Bible study is one of the best ways of sharing the Gospel with other families! Read the Bible, ask the four simple questions, and summarize the discussion! That's all you need to do in order to dig open a person's heart and plant the seed of God's Word!

Remember too, that all sharing is done sensitively. To share means to ask questions about the other people; it means to share in their concerns and problems, and we can do that only if we allow them to talk and tell us what is bothering them. Parents need to do this with children and with each other.

Reflect/Discuss:
How can we "share" more effectively with each other.

Meditate:
Questions are the "shovel" used to open the ground to plant God's Word in a heart.

DAY 40
Step #4:
Dare

When Jesus finished the Sermon on the Mount and, accompanied by a large crowd, came down the mountainside, a daring leper suddenly broke through the people and knelt before Jesus worshiping Him (see Matt. 8:1–4). He was daring for many reasons. Probably the most significant reason was the fact that he was in the crowd. Lepers were outcastes—cast out of any crowd to live "outside." Undoubtedly, many in the group were furious at the man's audacity in running up to Jesus.

But there is more. Jesus was attracting large crowds of people, and they were fascinated by what He said. And indeed, He had done some miracles. But the healing of a leper was a miracle no one had ever done. This man not only dared to incur the anger of the crowd, but he dared to thrust himself upon someone who had never healed a leper before.

Not only had Jesus not healed anyone before, He had never even promised to heal a leper! That's a third reason the man was so daring. He did not even have the promise of Christ's healing on which to base his radical appeal!

There is more to his daring, however. While daring, he is also humble. He doesn't demand to be healed. His is a humble request. He says, "If You want to You can heal me." He is coming in such great faith; he acknowledges that even if Jesus doesn't grant his request, it doesn't mean Jesus doesn't have the power to heal him.

He dares to come to Jesus because he has a profound faith in Him. Even though Jesus has not yet done this, he has faith that Jesus can do it, if He wants to. And in that faith he kneels before Christ and worships Him.

A humble daring. A faith-filled daring. But also, this leper is passionate. He feels so deeply about Christ's ability to cleanse him that he risks everything. He dares to break all regulations about being in a crowd. He dares to come to a man who has never healed a leper or even promised to heal one and in faith ask Him for cleansing.

This is the kind of daring we need in our homes. Is there any Christian home without some kind of "impossible" situation like the leper's situation? Somewhere in all of our relationships there is that "hopeless" situation. Do we dare to ask the Savior to heal it? Humbly ask Him? Ask Him in faith and confidence that if it suits His plan, He will heal it? If you are to have a true home of prayer every day, you must dare to bring the impossible things to God in prayer, trusting them to Him. Leave them with Him. Acknowledge that He looks at the problem from the eternal side, you only look at it from yesterday and today.

The B.L.E.S.S.ing

Jesus blessed the leper, transforming him in five ways. He touched his body, and his body was cleansed of the leprosy. That's what the man asked for. But in addition he got four more transformations. Because his body was healed, his labor was transformed. He was not confined any longer to begging, as were all the lepers of his day. He was whole. He would not contaminate other workers. He could work and find dignity and satisfaction.

Jesus transformed him in a third way. His emotions were changed. He went from the pit of despair to trembling hope and then to overwhelming joy as he realized how the Savior's touch had transformed him. His body, his labor, his emotions—all were instantly transformed.

He experienced a fourth transformation in his social relationships. He no longer had to live in the leper's camp outside the city. He was no longer an outcaste. He was whole, and the priest proclaimed him healed and opened the door for new social relationships as he reentered society.

The final transformation came in his spiritual relationship. He met the Savior, and I am confident, even though Matthew does not say this directly, that this man became a disciple of the Lord. Through faith the leper was transformed spiritually for eternity.

These five transformations spell B.L.E.S.S. He was transformed in his:

Body

Labor

Emotions

Social Relationships

Spiritual Life in Christ.

Dr. Alvin VanderGriend, who served Mission India as director of its initial H.O.P.E. ministries, developed this acronym B.L.E.S.S. He encouraged people to adopt five other families, praying for them five days per week, and asking for these five blessings as needed.

As you encourage your family to meet weekly—to pray, to share, to care—encourage them also to dream awesome dreams. Like the leper transformed by Christ, and with the same passion, trust, and humility, encourage each member not only to bring each other, but to bring five other families to Christ in prayer. Dare to dream that Christ could and would transform the five families, just as he transformed the leper years ago.

Reflect/Discuss:

*Will you ask God to make your home a **H**ome **O**f **P**rayer **E**very day? Will you get the family together, ask them to read these meditations and then set aside a special time on a regular schedule to meet in praise and petition? Will you encourage them to share with each other around God's Word and learn how to care and receive care equally from each other?*

Meditate:

"The truth is, anyone who believes in me will do the same works I have done, and even greater works, because I am going to be with the Father. You can ask for anything in my name, and I will do it, because the work of the Son brings glory to the Father. Yes, ask anything in my name, and I will do it" (John 14:12–14 NLT).

---

[1] If you are interested in receiving the free *India Intercessor* prayer letter, please contact Mission India using the information on the copyright page.

[2] If you are interested in the free *Rice Bag* project for your family, church or Sunday School, please contact Mission India using the information on the copyright page.

Dr. John DeVries has devoted his life to ministry and international missions. He has actively trained church leaders, adult literacy teachers, Bible school workers, pastors, and Bible teachers. He has led extensive ministry in India, where he has initiated prayer movements in each of that nation's 28 states.